THE ART OF THE MARKET

THE ART OF THE MARKET

TWO CENTURIES OF AMERICAN BUSINESS AS SEEN THROUGH ITS STOCK CERTIFICATES

Bob Tamarkin and Les Krantz

with commentary by George LaBarre

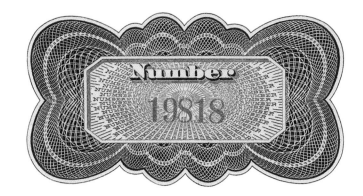

To Civia and Margie, our most valuable assets.

Published by Stewart, Tabori & Chang
A division of Harry N. Abrams, Inc.
115 West 18th Street
New York, NY 10011

The text of this book was composed in Adobe Minion,
captions were composed in Adobe Copperplate and Clarendon.
Printed and bound in Hong Kong by C&C Offset Printing Co. Ltd

Library of Congress Cataloging-in-Publication Data
Tamarkin, Bob.
    The art of the market: two centuries of American
       business as seen through its stock certificates / Bob
       Tamarkin and Les Krantz.
       p.   cm.
    Includes bibliographical references and index.
    ISBN 1-55670-938-2
    1.   Stock certificates—United States—History.
    2. Industries—United States—History.
    I. Krantz, Les. II. Title.
HG4633.T36   1999
332.63'22'0973—dc21   99-31562
                     CIP

10 9 8 7 6 5 4 3 2

C O N T E N T S

CAPITAL STOC

No. 28

United

INCOR

ROBERT

SIDNEY

JOSEPH

This Certifies that

of

OF BOSTON.

ASSISTANT CASHIER.

Sixty se

of the United

INTRODUCTION

Recently America's romance with the stock market reached a new milestone: For the first time total assets of mutual funds surpassed total assets of the nation's banks, inextricably linking Wall Street and Main Street. In total, stocks now represent a greater share of personal wealth than homes. In 1990, stock holdings of all kinds accounted for 21 percent of households' total financial assets. In 1998, the share had doubled to 42 percent. The momentum in stock buying carried over into 1999 as the Dow Jones industrial average soared beyond the 10,000 barrier for the first time. Along the continuum of economic history, it seems, the public has been only too eager to buy a share of capitalism. Today in the United States alone, there are nearly 70 million direct owners of corporate shares and stock mutual funds, in addition to 133 million other individuals who own stock indirectly through such assets as life insurance portfolios, pension plans, mutual savings banks, and college endowment funds.

Oddly enough, as more Americans are relating to the stock market (whether or not they understand its dynamics), fewer of them will be able to relate to stock certificates, those adorned pieces of paper that—in the age of cyberspace transactions by which a stock certificate is replaced by a so-called electronic book entry—are destined to become financial artifacts, like ancient coins found among ruins that give insight into the nature of a culture.

What is a stock certificate anyway? There are, of course, the physical components: paper, ink, and small engraved pictures called vignettes. And the metaphysical: faith in the underlying value. Simply, a stock certificate is a bill of sale—proof of part ownership and the extent of that ownership in a corporation.

OPPOSITE: VIGNETTES WITH ALLEGORICAL FIGURES POISED NEXT TO AN AMERICAN BALD EAGLE DECORATED MANY NINETEENTH- AND EARLY TWENTIETH-CENTURY STOCK CERTIFICATES SUCH AS THIS UNITED STATES MINING COMPANY'S STOCK CIRCA 1900. COURTESY OF GEORGE HEWITSON COLLECTIBLES.

Say, for example, that there are a million shares of company XYZ. If you owned one share of the company, you'd own one-millionth of the company and have a claim on one-millionth of its profits. So that ownership, called equity, carries with it expectation. Some people buy stocks to get income from the dividends, a share of the company's net profits after expenses and taxes have been deducted. (The dividend is paid in a fixed amount for each share of stock held and, unlike interest on a debt, dividends must be voted on by the company's directors before each payment.) Others buy stocks with the anticipation that the value of the stock will go up over time and they can sell it at a higher price than they bought it for to make a profit. Some companies pay dividends in stock rather than in cash. For years, Archer Daniels Midland, for example, paid an annual dividend of 5 percent; each shareholder was given five extra shares for every one hundred shares owned. Other companies send samples of their products to shareholders as a form of dividend. While most companies pay dividends, there are those who don't. Instead, they plow money back into the company for new products, research, or other ventures that will help the company grow. Still other companies pay no dividends because they have no profits.

A stock is different than a bond, which basically is a loan—an IOU—to an issuer like a corporation or a federal, state, or local government or agency. Like a stock issue the object is the same: to raise money. A bond certificate shows the amount loaned, the rate of interest to be paid on the loan, and the date the principal will be repaid. In 1792, the first five securities traded in New York City were three government bonds and two bank notes. But a stock certificate is far more than a financial instrument. It's the hinge on which the doors of a corporation open to strangers, so long as they can pony up the entrance fee.

Behind the stock certificate there's the aura of history and art. And lure. A pitch that you, too, can have a piece of the action in someone's dream. It's a piece of risk, a bet placed with others in capitalistic enterprise. The certificate, in a sense, is a marriage contract between an individual and industry that share mutual values— the concern for chasing and making a dollar.

Moreover, stock certificates tell a tale of progress; sometimes it's a fool's tale, but more often it's a glorious one—of a paper trail whose indelible imprints snake through the eras of American history with its wars, panics, peace, and prosperity. Stock certificates are the caviar of financial instruments, like paper money, grandfathered into our financial DNA.

Certificates can also be seen as time capsules. For even though a company may go belly up or be gobbled into the belly of another, losing its identity completely, the stock certificate itself remains. It can be a vivid reminder of corporate America's mortality, while it fends off a company's oblivion.

No wonder there are growing legions of scripophiles—collectors of stocks and bonds—in practically every corner of the world. Not only are they drawn by the signatures of renowned magnates and politicians on these certificates, but also by the classic vignettes of allegorical figures that blend mythology with industry, commerce, trade, agriculture, and historical events created by America's greatest engravers and artists going back to the eighteenth century. (Scripophiles are discussed in further detail in Chapter 2.)

To really understand what a stock certificate is, however, it's necessary to understand that for a stock to be a stock it must be backed up by something tangible. Long before smog and acid rain, when the great smoking chimneys of factories and trains polluted the air for the good of mankind, corporations took pride in rendering industrial scenes on their stock certificates. Others, however, tried to bring their gigantic proportions down to scale with rustic images and pastoral scenes, conveying a friendly tone. Factories, trains, steamships, automobiles, airplanes, bridges, mine shafts, steel mills, oil derricks, transmitting towers, and forests intermingled with gods and goddesses to create images of power, progress, and stability. Such fanciful illustrations on stock certificates encouraged investors to part with their money on more than one occasion.

Magnifying industry's pollution as something wonderful would, of course, change over the decades as corporations grew environmentally sensitive and politically correct. Social conscience affected the design and look of stock certificates that fluctuated like the markets themselves. Early certificates were usually one color and rather austere in design, presenting an archetypal

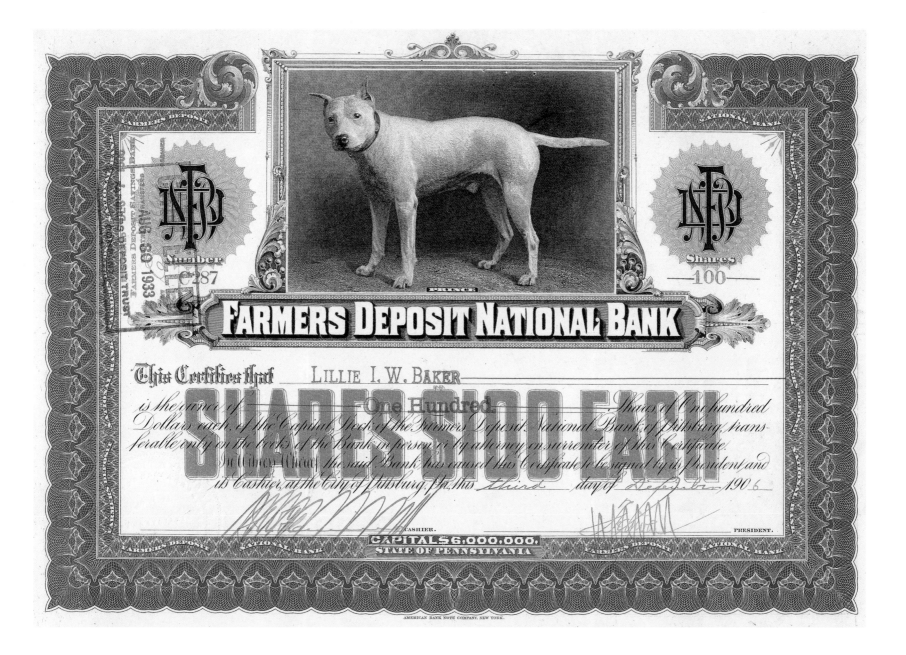

FARMERS DEPOSIT NATIONAL BANK

ABOVE: ONE OF THE MOST ENDEARING PETS THAT EVER GRACED THE FACE OF A STOCK CERTIFICATE WAS PRINCE, WHOSE MASTER WAS PRESIDENT OF FARMERS DEPOSIT NATIONAL BANK IN PITTSBURGH. THE DOG WOULD ACCOMPANY HIM TO WORK DAILY AND IN TIME BECAME THE CORPORATE SYMBOL, APPEARING ON THE BANK'S LETTERHEAD AND CHECKS AS WELL. THIS TERRIER BREED, SHOWN HERE ON A CERTIFICATE FROM THE 1900S, HAD A REPUTATION FOR BEING A TENACIOUS WATCHDOG. *PRINCE* WAS ENGRAVED BY ROBERT SAVAGE FOR AMERICAN BANK NOTE COMPANY. COURTESY OF GEORGE LABARRE.

OPPOSITE: REVENUE STAMPS LIKE THE THREE SHOWN HERE WERE AFFIXED ON THE FACE OF FINANCIAL DOCUMENTS SUCH AS CHECKS, DEEDS, STOCKS, AND BONDS AS A TAX TO HELP FINANCE THE CIVIL WAR.

view. Industry and commerce were given literal meaning in design. A railroad featured a train; a turnpike, a road; a canal, a waterway. In fact, most of the stock certificates prior to about 1835 were minimalist in nature with few vignettes. As for color, they were more in line with Ford's Model T—black only, thank you. After the Civil War, however, as business boomed color and complexity were incorporated in the certificates, if for no other reason than to fend off counterfeiters. By the late nineteenth century, blue, green, brown, orange, and red along with black were splashed over certificates. By the Gilded Age—the period roughly between the end of the Civil War and the late 1890s—stock design had become flamboyant, even gaudy, to mirror the era.

As times and the industrial mix changed so did the certificates. Like the skin-and-bones architecture that dominated big city skylines in the twentieth century, some certificates again became functional, boring, hardly reflective of the dynamic personalities of a company's founder. For instance, the common share certificate of auto maker Tucker Corporation, issued in 1947, is as spare as it gets: entirely in script with no vignette and a modest border. Reminiscent of one of those standard fill-in-the-blank leases, the Tucker certificate looks like the stationery store certificates in lithographed form that were produced by New York's Goes Publishing Company and Chicago's Dwight & M. H. Jackson, a division of Corporation Supply Company. At the other extreme, some modern-day certificates exploded in color like that of the Disney Corporation, whose founder Walt Disney is flanked by Mickey Mouse, Donald Duck, and his other creations. And the garish Ringling Brothers–Barnum & Bailey Circus certificate that screams four-color showmanship from the high wire to the sawdust-covered floor of the big top.

For many shareholders, the vignette on the face of a stock certificate that depicted a corporation's business was the nearest they came to seeing their investments. It was intended to provide a sense of closeness to the corporation, like words and pictures in an exhibit. The face of a stock certificate was narcissistic in that it was the corporation's best face, its no-nonsense business face. That was especially true before mass advertising and corporate public relations created an image that institutions, rather than mere factories, manufactured products. That's why the faces of founders whose companies bore their names sometimes graced their stock certificates, too. A sampling of the engraved portraits: A somber and coifed Mary Kay, founder of Mary Kay Cosmetics (engraved by Kenneth Guy, one of the twentieth century's preeminent engravers); a smiling and perky Jenny Craig, queen of weight-reducing programs (engraved by Armandina Lozano, America's only female portrait engraver); a matronly and bespectacled Fanny Farmer, whose homemade fudge became the featured product sold by Fanny Farmer Candy Shops Inc. (engraved by British-born John Hay); and a bearded and stern James Garfield, the assassinated president who had founded the Garfield & Cherry Grove Rail Road (engraved by George Frederick Smillie, who was chief engraver of the U.S. Bureau of Engraving and Printing until 1922). Occasionally a CEO has been known to substitute the face of a family member for his own. The Farmers Deposit Bank of Pittsburgh stock certificate issued in 1910, for example, has at its center a portrait of Prince, a doughty English bull terrier that just happened to be the bank president's dog.

Like a memoir, stock certificates are self-serving. Why would they be otherwise? A certificate was fashioned to enhance a corporation's reputation by rendering it in the present and even providing a glimpse of its future as well. Back in 1898, for example, following the Great Blizzard of 1888 that swept through New York downing the ganglia of wires that hung between its buildings like jungle vines, the North American Underground Telegraph and Electric Company turned its stock certificate into an advertising poster of sorts. On its certificate of January 31, 1898, North American shrewdly depicted two scenes that told two different stories. The first scene was a vignette of a busy city street cluttered with telephone poles and wires that knitted the buildings together and nearly blocked out the sky. The other scene showed the same busy street without the unsightly wires. And in place of telephone poles that reached upward like reeds in a pond, there stood a row of trees under an open sky. In the foreground of the second vignette are workers underground laying the cable. The certificate clearly conveys the positive impact North American considered itself having on society.

Thus the stock certificate was corporate America's calling card—financial document, advertising pitch, and public relations ploy all rolled into one—designed to grab the individual as an investor and perhaps even as a consumer who would use the company's product. As a tool of a corporation's expression and relevance, the stock certificate is like a painting or photograph that bears the marks of singular sensibility. Sometimes a certificate rendered the company in its youthful, formative, uncertain stage; sometimes in its middle age of reconstruction; and sometimes in its old age of custom. Its market value notwithstanding, the certificate is a reminder that all companies go through cycles and need transfusions of capital by either borrowing or selling securities at various stages of their lives. Make no mistake, despite satirist Ambrose Bierce's definition of a corporation as "an ingenious device for obtaining individual profit without individual responsibility," a corporation is a "legal person" that often outlives its original shareholders, managers, and employees, according to finance professors Richard A. Brealey of the London Business School and Stewart C. Myers of M.I.T.'s Sloan School of Management. They cite Chief Justice John Marshall's interpretation of a corporation written in 1819: "A corporation is an artificial being, invisible, intangible, and existing only in contemplation of law...it possesses only those properties which the charter of its creation confers upon it.... Among the most important are immortality,

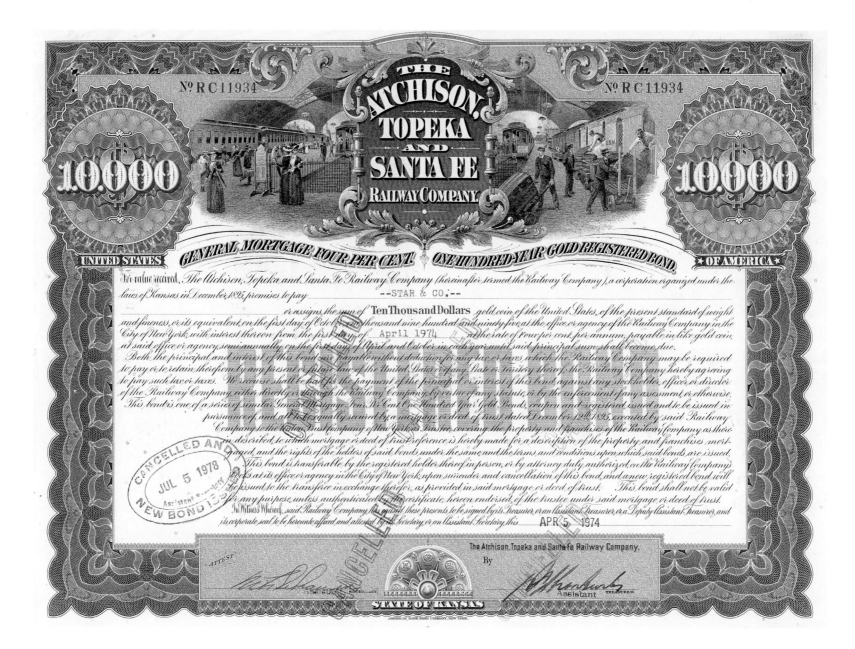

THE ATCHISON, TOPEKA AND SANTA FE RAILWAY COMPANY

ABOVE AND OPPOSITE: NOT MANY RAILROADS HAVE AN OSCAR-WINNING SONG WRITTEN ABOUT THEM. THE SONG TITLED "THE ATCHISON TOPEKA AND THE SANTA FE" WAS SUNG BY JUDY GARLAND IN *THE HARVEY GIRLS*. THE ATCHISON TOPEKA AND SANTA FE RAILWAY COMPANY WAS CHARTERED IN 1859 TO CONNECT ATCHINSON AND TOPEKA, KANSAS. MEANWHILE THE SANTA FE EXPANDED EASTWARD TO CHICAGO, WESTWARD TO THE PACIFIC COAST, AND SOUTHWARD TO THE GULF OF MEXICO. THE VIGNETTE ON THIS GENERAL MORTGAGE BOND (1974) IS OF A SANTA FE DEPOT ENGRAVED BY EDWIN GUNN AND CHARLES SKINNER FOR AMERICAN BANK NOTE. COURTESY OF GEORGE LABARRE.

Nº RC 11934

$10,000

UNITED STATES

GENERAL MORTGAGE FOUR PER

For value received, The Atchison, Topeka and Santa Fe Railwa

laws of Kansas in December, 1895, promises to pay _____

_____ or assigns, the sum of Te

and fineness, or its equivalent, on the first day of October, one thou

City of New York, with interest thereon from the first day of _____

at said office or agency, semi-annually on the first days of April

Both the principal and interest of this bond are payable w

to pay or to retain therefrom by any present or future law of the

to pay such tax or taxes. No recourse shall be had for the paym

and, if the expression may be allowed, individuality; properties, by which a perpetual succession of many persons are considered as the same, and may act as a single individual. They enable a corporation to manage its own affairs….By these means, a perpetual succession of individuals are capable of action for the promotion of the particular object, like one immortal being."

In any case, the stock certificate imparts consciousness at a level that is both practical and intellectual, synonymously tying an investor's financial destiny to a corporation's. The certificate was a kind of subliminal seducer, along the lines of a "hidden persuader," the term Vance Packard tagged advertisements with in the late 1950s. After all, a stock certificate was designed to portray something risky and speculative as solid. Why else would the Great Republic Gold and Silver Mining Company stock certificate display portraits of Queen Victoria and Abraham Lincoln? Obviously, the stock's promoters were hoping to snag investors from both sides of the Atlantic. Americans, subconsciously, often equate biggest and most powerful with best— big trains, big ships, big mills, big business.

As the investment culture intensified, a striving for status developed and encouraged the notion that prosperity was helping to achieve the dream of a classless, egalitarian society. But, ironically, stock category implied class. Some corporations issue different classes of stock, each with its own privilege. Common stock, for example, may be designated as class A or B or preferred. The A class—usually reserved for the founders—may have controlling voting rights. But both A and B may share equally in dividends. The preferred stock, on the other hand, is the blue blood of the group, bred with the characteristics of a stock and a bond. Preferred shareholders have first claim on dividends over that of common shareholders and on assets as well if the company dissolves. Like a bond, a preferred share pays a fixed dividend at the time of issuance. Unlike bondholders' claims, however, preferred shareholders' claims are not legally enforceable. Depending on a corporation's financial structure, trying to figure out its classes of stock can be reminiscent of Abbott and Costello's "Who's On First?" routine. At one time, for example, the highly diversified International Telephone & Telegraph Corp. had no less than eleven different preferred stocks among its issues of securities.

So a stock certificate (unlike a book entry) is tangible evidence of the fact that the holder has invested money in a given company and defines the extent of the holdings against those of fellow-shareholders. Certificates can be touched, stacked, fondled, tucked away in a vault or safety deposit box with stamps, coins, deeds, wills, and other odds and ends. It has real, intrinsic, and psychic value. Some stock certificates were meant to be compelling, inspiring, even patriotic. These adorned pieces of paper seemed to say, Support American progress by buying a share in the future of capitalism. That's why many of them display an American flag, an American eagle, and the faces of American presidents. Thus a stock certificate tugs partly at emotion, partly at reason, and, most certainly at greed. Bullish is good. Buy. Buy. In the late 1800s, when the nation's commodity exchanges were gearing up and the railroads were bolting westward, to be a risk-taker was patriotic, Darwinian, and quite in character with the psychology of an expansion-minded America playing out its "manifest destiny" with an unbridled zeal for ships, colonies, and power.

A stock certificate, by its nature, conveys a sense of motion—movement forward, upward, outward—an economic universe expanding. The perception carries with it a psychic value similar to that of money. In

SOUTHERN BELL TELEPHONE AND TELEGRAPH COMPANY

1971, for example, the United States closed the gold window to bring an end to the Bretton Woods agreement, which fixed exchange rates to an anemic gold standard. Before 1971, the value of money had been linked in the mind of the beholder to a commodity of some kind or another—from feathers in Brazil to hubcap-sized stones on the island of Yap. The Japanese had used iron as a monetary standard during the nineteenth century. The Western world, too, had metals mania, as summed up by Karl Marx: "Money is, by nature, gold and silver." Until the administration of Lyndon Johnson, the American dollar bill carried the legend, "Payable in silver to the bearer on demand."

Economist and Nobel laureate Paul A. Samuelson was once asked why gold goes up.

ABOVE: ALLEGORICAL FIGURES FLANK THE DESK TELEPHONE, INTRODUCED IN 1928, ON THE VIGNETTE OF A SOUTHERN BELL TELEPHONE AND TELEGRAPH BOND. COURTESY GEORGE LABARRE.

His reply: "Because it goes up! Why does it go down? Because it does." Sometimes stocks move the same way, ignoring the fundamentals while giving in to mass psychology, whether it be sparked by inflation or deflation or the panic of sellers or the euphoria of buyers. That's why the art of prediction falls short in trying to pick a market's direction or foretell when a particular stock will spiral upward or downward. Yet people are constantly looking for patterns and

rules that define the game and lay out its odds, hoping to become the Hoyle of the stock market. And that's why perception counts. "Money," wrote George Simmel in *The Philosophy of Money*, "is similar to the forms of logic, which lend themselves equally to any particular content, regardless of that content's development or combination."

Britain adopted the gold standard in 1816, but it carried no weight along the coast of Guinea in Africa, where all the gold bullion in the world couldn't buy a spear. However, a string of cowrie beads could. Some tribes of Native Americans used wampum, small beads made of shells (a black or dark purple bead was worth twice as much as a white one), and the early settlers in Virginia used tobacco to stoke their pipe dreams of wealth. Tobacco money was revived after World War II ended in Europe when American G.I.s bought almost anything they wanted with packs of Camels and Lucky Strikes in the ravaged countries they occupied. As in prisons, cigarette currency became the main monetary exchange.

There were, of course, blips in the panorama of monetary history when governments cranked out irredeemable paper money with nothing more than a prayer, if that, behind it. During the Revolutionary War, for example, the Continental Congress switched from coin, or specie, to paper money, and the new currency dropped in value faster than the temperature at Valley Forge. It depreciated so quickly that the phrase "not worth a continental" became synonymous with worthlessness in the American lexicon. In the second year of the Civil War, to avoid bankruptcy, the North printed large quantities of greenbacks, paper money that was green on the back, and declared them legal tender for debts. Six months later, they weren't worth a continental, and the Lincoln administration was forced to levy new taxes on manufactured goods and income taxes on railroad and steamship companies, along with a tax on financial transactions that involved checks, claims, deeds, stocks, and bonds (a revenue stamp was affixed to the face of the particular document to show that the tax was paid).

In essence a stock certificate, like paper money, is nothing more than a symbol of wealth backed by the faith of its investor in the future. A person doesn't buy a stock to get last year's dividends, but to get future dividends. "And when you look at the stock of the General Electric Company you will not find its 'real value' in the stock certificate," states John Magee in *The General Semantics of Wall Street*. "Nor in Schenectady, nor Lynn, nor any other property of the General Electric Company. The 'real value' of that stock is entirely a matter of what it is worth to somebody." Not surprising, the feel and look of stock certificates would take on the cachet of money. Like feathers and colored beads and intricately designed bank notes—paper money—that caught the eye and the confidence of their users, stock certificates, too, would acquire their own festooned charm with intaglio-engraved vignettes, medallions, rosettes, and scrolls bathed in an autumnal palette of colors. At times unauthorized stock—like counterfeit bills—was sold as gilt-edged securities. Which meant they also weren't worth a continental. Their value had dropped along with the investor's faith in corporate America and its banking system. "Buy! Buy!" became "Sell! Sell!" The phrase "plaster the wall with worthless stock certificates" grew out of the crash of 1929. The stock market has always been fertile ground for plungers, insiders, and schemers, luring, then fleecing the public and each other.

Like paper money, stock certificates are destined to become obsolete. The use of plastic money—charge cards and credit cards and ATM cards—already suggest we are headed for a cashless society. Can a certificateless society be far behind? For instance, most owners of mutual funds—there are more than 100 million mutual fund accounts in the United States—receive no certificates at all. Instead, proof of ownership is a confirmation of sale called a book entry—a security for which the buyer receives a receipt rather than an engraved certificate.

Given their rich history, it would be a shame if stock certificates were replaced by electronic expediency. Writing in *Institutional Investor*, Claire Makin wryly concluded: "Stock certificates were abstractions, but peculiarly tangible and human ones; digital accounts entombed in computer memories, though convenient, lack a certain romance."

NUMBER

141

CAPITAL STOCK
$2,000,000

SHARES

INCORPORATED UNDER THE LAWS
OF THE STATE OF PENNSYLVANIA

ALLEGHENY VALLEY STREET RAILWAY COMPANY

This Certifies that C. C. Gerwig is entitled to _____ Shares of the fully paid Capital Stock of the Allegheny Valley Street Railway Company transferable only on the books of the Company in person or by Attorney on surrender of this Certificate. This Certificate is not valid until countersigned and registered by the Registrar of Transfers. Witness the seal of the said Company, attested by the signatures of its President and Treasurer this _____ day of _____ 1906

TREASURER

PRESIDENT

ALLEGHENY VALLEY STREET RAILWAY COMPANY

ABOVE: THE ALLEGHENY VALLEY STREET RAILWAY COMPANY WAS FORMED IN 1906 THROUGH CONSOLIDATION OF PITTSBURGH'S HARMAR STREET RAILWAY, O'HARA STREET RAILWAY, AND THE TARENTUM TRACK PASS RAILWAY. THE STREET RAILWAY RAN 20 MILES, TRANSPORTING NEARLY 1.5 MILLION PASSENGERS A YEAR. THE LINE WAS RUN BY MELLONS (SEE SIGNATURES). PRESIDENT WILLIAM LANIER MELLON WAS THE NEPHEW OF ALLEGHENY'S TREASURER, RICHARD BEATTY MELLON, WHO SUCCEEDED HIS BROTHER, THE RENOWNED ANDREW, AS PRESIDENT OF THE MELLON NATIONAL BANK OF PITTSBURGH. COURTESY OF GEORGE LABARRE.

ia,

EREBY CERTIFIED, by the Pres.

f the Philadelphia and Lancaster

Thomas Willing

he City of Philadelphia

e share of Stock, in the said Company, nu

d twenty five

tr

There's always been romance in risky ventures that promise a return. In 1580, Queen Elizabeth I was a major shareholder in the syndicate that financed Sir Francis Drake's expedition against Spain from which he loaded the Golden Hind with treasure. Out of her share she paid off all of England's foreign debt, balanced its budget, and was left with a surplus, which she promptly invested in the Levant Company, an overseas trading concern. With the sizable profits from the Levant venture, the East India Company, which became the springboard of England's colonial empire, was founded. Queen Elizabeth certainly knew how to parlay her winnings and in the process gave a boost to the joint-stock enterprise, the forerunner of the modern corporation.

THE BIRTH OF THE SHARE

In a joint-stock company (now virtually an obsolete term) capital was divided into small units, permitting a number of investors to contribute varying amounts to the total. Profits were divided between stockholders in proportion to the number of shares they owned. These joint-stock ventures developed in the seventeenth century as a means to pool large amounts of capital to finance such costly enterprises as overseas trading companies. (In 1601, the word "share" tied to capital investment first appears in the English language in connection with the joint-stock company, according to the *Oxford English Dictionary*. The original meaning of "stock" referred to the trunk of a tree, which implies foundation or outgrowth. As early as 1463, "stock" shows up as a sum of money set aside and in 1526 as capital to trade or to invest

with. The term "stockbroker," a dealer in stocks, was first used in 1706. But the term "stock bill"—the forerunner of the stock certificate—wasn't used until 1760.)

In 1607, English merchants and emigrants formed a joint-stock company to establish Jamestown, America's first settlement. By 1695, there were ninety-three joint-stock companies in England. A wave of economic cycles reduced the number of stockholder companies to just twenty-one by 1721, following

OPPOSITE: THE PHILADELPHIA AND LANCASTER TURNPIKE ROAD (1795) IS ONE OF THE MOST FAMOUS EARLY SHARES. PRINTED ON VELLUM, IT IS SIGNED BY WILLIAM BINGHAM, A WELL-KNOWN FINANCIER AND PUBLIC FIGURE IN PENNSYLVANIA. COURTESY OF RICHARD GREGG.

Philadelphia, March 16th 1795

BE IT HEREBY CERTIFIED, by the President, Managers, and Company of the **Philadelphia** and **Lancaster** Turnpike Road, that

N.º 1075

Thomas Willing of the City of Philadelphia is entitled to one share of Stock in the said Company, numbered One thousand and Twenty five transferrable in the Presence of the President or Treasurer, by the said Thomas Willing or his Attorney, Agreeably to an Act of the General Assembly of the Commonwealth of Pennsylvania, passed the Tenth Day of April, in the Year of our Lord One thousand Seven Hundred and Ninety two, and the Charter of said Company. Sealed with the common Seal of the said Company.

_____ Treasurer. W. Bingham President.

PHILADELPHIA AND LANCASTER TURNPIKE ROAD

ABOVE: IN 1795, WILLIAM BINGHAM SOLD STOCK TO HELP FINANCE THE PRIVATELY BUILT PHILADELPHIA AND LANCASTER TURNPIKE ROAD, WHICH RAN 62 MILES. THE COST WAS A HEFTY $465,000, AND SHAREHOLDERS WERE TO BE PAID A RETURN ON THEIR INVESTMENT OUT OF THE PROFITS FROM TOLL FEES. THE ABOVE PHILADELPHIA AND LANCASTER TURNPIKE ROAD SHARE CERTIFICATE DATED 1795 IS THE EARLIEST KNOWN SHARE IN AMERICA TO USE A VIGNETTE. THE SHARE IS SIGNED BY BINGHAM, WHO WAS A DIRECTOR OF AMERICA'S FIRST BANK, THE BANK OF NORTH AMERICA (CHARTERED IN 1781) AND FOUNDER OF BINGHAMTON, NEW YORK. COURTESY OF RICHARD GREGG.

Nº 93 James Hopkins ——— is entitled to One Share in the Stock of the PRESIDENT, MANAGERS, & COMPANY of RANCOCUS TOLL-BRIDGE. WITNESS, the Signatures of the *President* and *Treasurer*, and the Seal of the said Corporation, the *eighteenth* Day of *February* 1793. *Joshua M. Wallace* PRESIDENT. *Countersigned by William Cote jun* TREASURER.

the South Sea Bubble fiasco in 1720. A stockbroker and his colleague had talked the British government into converting its short-term war debts into equity in a new joint-stock company called the South Sea Company, which was given a monopoly on English trade with Spain. The public also invested in the new venture, feeling secure because the enterprise was government sanctioned. After a decade, however, the company's financial machinations and the public's wild speculation caused its stock to blow up like a bubble (at one point it rose from 128 pounds a share to 1,000 in seven months). Finally the speculative bubble burst and the stock plummeted, leaving scores of bleeding investors. And thus the South Sea Bubble secured its place in history as part of a chain link in financial disasters. Who were the investors back then? In *The South Sea Bubble* Viscount Erleigh defined them and explored how greed overtook their speculative souls: "Statesmen forgot their Politics, Lawyers the Bar, Merchants their Traffic, Physicians their Patients, Tradesmen their Shops, Debtors of Quality their Creditors, Divines the Pulpit, and even the Women themselves their Pride and Vanity!"

Out of an informal patchwork of exchanges in London coffeehouses the British Stock Exchange was founded in 1773. It provided a central marketplace for buying and selling stocks in all kinds of new enterprises spurred by the Industrial Revolution. By the late eighteenth century the small island nation, which controlled the seas, was literally under a cloud of soot from the huffing smokestacks in a place known as Coalbrookdale, where the alchemy of iron, steel, and coal forged the great Iron Bridge. Mechanical power had replaced animal power. From the sweat and muscle of this Dickensian era also came a sobering fact: Many investors—like those who backed the trading companies—were needed to finance the new industrial machine.

In America—still mostly an untracked continent—nearly 90 percent of the population were farmers, most of them eking out a bare subsistence or struggling to sell their

ABOVE: THE RANCOCUS TOLL-BRIDGE (1793) IS A PRIMITIVE CERTIFICATE. TO PROTECT AGAINST COUNTERFEITING, THE SIGNATURES WERE EXECUTED WITH A QUILL TIP. IT IS A LESS THAN FOOLPROOF METHOD, YET EFFECTIVE ENOUGH FOR THE TIME. COURTESY OF RICHARD GREGG.

commodities abroad. By 1787, America's post-revolutionary economic slump was slowly abating. Even before America's new government was set up in 1789, Alexander Hamilton advised Americans to scrap household industries. Trade in local self-sufficiency for the national exchange of commodities, he urged. By the early decades of the nineteenth century a new society was emerging out of a colonial past. An urban working class was slowly forming. The sons and daughters of farm families fled to the cities for factory jobs that produced textiles, shoes, hardware, iron, leather, and whiskey. The towns became the new frontiers just as they had in Europe. The turnpikes and new means of transportation beckoned investors, of which there was no shortage.

The Puritans, it turned out, had brought with them to the New World not only an appetite for turkey, but for risk as well. (Not surprising, since the fact that they braved the Atlantic for the unknown indeed showed a risky spirit.) The very roots of America were based on a gamble. The thirteen original colonies were financed largely by lotteries, as were such schools as Harvard, Yale, Princeton, Brown, Dartmouth, and Columbia. George Washington and Benjamin Franklin were staunch advocates of lotteries as a means of raising public funds. Agrarian Thomas Jefferson, who conceded the need for domestic manufacturers, went so far as to endorse the lottery as "a salutary instrument wherein the tax is laid on the willing only."

Risk, then, was already a part of America's economic fabric and helped to stimulate the flurry of joint-stock companies that were founded in the 1790s, including the first mechanically powered cotton mill used by Almy, Brown and Slatersland in 1793. A year earlier, when rivers, canals, and turnpikes were the chief avenues of trade, the New York Stock Exchange was organized. (In 1817, New York stockbrokers chartered a formal organization to adopt rules for the conduct of business. They called it the New York Stock & Exchange Board [NYS&EB] and rented a room at 40 Wall Street.) There were, of course, no railroads, telegraphs, or telephones and the post office in 1800—with five million Americans scattered over a big country—handled some three million letters, less than one per person per year. People, goods, ideas, and news traveled very slowly. To speed things up, in 1795 Pennsylvania financier William Bingham proposed building the sixty-two-mile-long Philadelphia and Lancaster Turnpike. He turned to the public for help, selling shares in the venture to raise $465,000, a sizable sum at the time. Investors would be paid back with the profits collected from the turnpike tolls. Not only was it the first such toll road in the United States, but historians believe that the share certificates carried the first

LEFT: PORTRAIT OF ALEXANDER HAMILTON (1755–1804), U.S. STATESMAN. COURTESY OF AMERICAN BANK NOTE COMPANY.

No 64, representing 5 shares from 566 to 570.

This is to Certify, that James Greenleaf is entitled to five ————— Shares in the entire Property of the **NORTH AMERICAN LAND COMPANY**, the Dividend whereof shall not be less than **Six Dollars**, on each Share Annually, conformably to Articles of Agreement Duly Executed, dated at **PHILADELPHIA** the twentieth day of February 1795. Transferable only at the Company's Office in that **CITY**, by the Owner in Person, or by his Executor, Administrator, Attorney, or Legal Representative. Signed in the presence, and by Order of the Board of Managers, at Philadelphia, this tenth day of March One thousand seven hundred and ninety five.

James Marshall Secretary   Rob Morris, President.

NORTH AMERICAN LAND COMPANY

ABOVE: THE NORTH AMERICAN LAND COMPANY WAS FORMED IN 1795 BY ROBERT MORRIS, WHO HAD MANAGED THE FINANCES OF THE AMERICAN COLONIES DURING THE REVOLUTIONARY WAR, IN AN EFFORT TO CAPITALIZE WESTWARD EXPANSION. NOT ONLY DOES MORRIS'S SIGNATURE APPEAR ON THE CERTIFICATE SHOWN ABOVE, BUT HE WAS ALSO ONE OF THE SIGNERS OF THE DECLARATION OF INDEPENDENCE. IN 1781 HE ORGANIZED THE BANK OF NORTH AMERICA—THE COUNTRY'S FIRST BANK—TO HELP GIVE SOLID BACKING TO PAPER MONEY. AT ONE TIME HIS CREDIT LINE EXCEEDED THAT OF THE ENTIRE YOUNG NATION, YET IN 1806 HE DIED IN POVERTY. COURTESY OF RICHARD GREGG.

vignette—a horse-drawn covered wagon moving down a road toward a gate—which was finely engraved on vellum.

Risk, of course, went hand in hand with speculation; and, as noted, it was not above the nation's founding fathers. After all, to start a revolution was a pretty risky venture in itself. But not every rainbow led to a pot of gold. Consider the misfortunes of Robert Morris, an early-American entrepreneur with a gilt-edged pedigree, who was one of the major financiers of the American Revolution, a signer of the Declaration of Independence, and a dear friend of George Washington. Before serving as a U.S. senator from Pennsylvania from 1789 to 1795, Morris had founded and organized the Bank of North America, whose stockholders included Thomas Jefferson, Alexander Hamilton, Benjamin Franklin, and James Monroe. Who wouldn't have invested in shares of his North American Land Company? So American was he that on a certificate commemorating the birth of the stars and stripes—issued by the American Flag House and the Betsy Ross Memorial Association—gazing in awe over the shoulder of Betsy Ross, who is busily sewing, are George Washington and his pal, Robert Morris. In 1789, Morris and John Nicholson formed the Asylum Company to provide refuge in America for the French nobility escaping the guillotine during the French Revolution. Unfortunately, not enough of the nobility got away and Morris was left holding big chunks of western land that had dropped in value because of lack of demand. He, along with his investors, lost a fortune. Broke and his reputation sullied, Morris eventually ended up in debtors' prison and died in 1806.

The young nation's first major securities speculator was also well connected. He was William Duer, assistant secretary of the treasury under Alexander Hamilton. In early 1790, Duer resigned his post when the government moved from New York to Philadelphia, and he turned from dabbling to serious speculation in stocks, land, manufacturing ventures, and even European deals. "Had he succeeded in all these activities," noted Robert Sobel in *Panic On Wall Street*, "he would have emerged as the most important businessman in America, and its most powerful until the days of J. P. Morgan." Duer's wild speculation, primarily in banking stocks—including the Bank of New York and the Bank of United States launched by Hamilton to guarantee the public credit—ended in disaster. Not even his association with Hamilton (who was accused by his detractors of a conflict of interest in trying to rescue Duer from his financial bind) could save him from debtors' prison, where he died in 1799.

In the nineteenth century, speculation flourished well beyond Wall Street. In the aftermath of the War of 1812, the market for securities began to grow. Along with government bonds, bank and insurance stocks began trading. While southerners were tying their fortunes to the production of cotton, following the opening of the Erie Canal, eastern land speculators swarmed over the West like locusts in a cotton field. They bought up every acre they could get their hands on, using the eastern bankers to finance their binge. Land values soared. In 1830, the first railroad stock, Mohawk and Hudson, was traded on the New York Stock Exchange.

WHERE DO BULLS AND BEARS COME FROM?

If you believe the stock market is rising, and you buy stocks hoping to sell them at a higher price, you are a bull. According to the *Dictionary of Modern Economics*, the term "bull" dates back to the eighteenth century, when dealers on the London Stock Exchange were called bulls if they thought the trend of stock and bond prices was up and "bears" if they thought it was down. Though no one knows for sure, the word could refer to the way a bull tosses things upward with its horns to describe the action of the bull on the exchange. Or as something that has the strength and power to move forward relatively unencumbered. A bear, on the other hand, is the pessimist who believes prices are going lower. Thus his or her strategy is the opposite to that of a bull's. Instead of buying, the bear sells short by borrowing the stock with hopes of buying it back at a lower price. The word bear also took root on the eighteenth-century London Stock Exchange. Back then there was an old proverb circulating on the exchange floor, "to sell a bear's skin before one caught the bear" described what the bear on the stock exchange does. The short-seller does not own the stock he is selling, but he borrows it, which brings to mind a second possibility for the origin of bear. It may be a perversion of the word "bare," in that the bear seller is bare of the securities he has sold.

BELOW: FORMED AS A CONSOLIDATION OF FOUR RAIL COMPANIES IN 1870, THE MISSOURI KANSAS AND TEXAS RAILWAY COMPANY (1889) OPERATED 1,386 MILES OF TRACK FROM HANNIBAL, MISSOURI, TO TAYLOR, TEXAS. COURTESY OF R.M. SMYTHE & CO, INC.

Railroad securities would come to dominate trading for the remainder of the century. The banks boomed, too. Between 1829 and 1837 the number of banks in the United States grew from 329 to 788. Now Americans were into chasing the dollar wherever it led them. "In a former age," mused Ralph Waldo Emerson in 1834, "men of might were men of will; now they are men of wealth." (Thirty years later Emerson would end up with one of America's wealthiest sons-in-law when his daughter, Edith, married Colonel William H. Forbes, president of Bell Telephone, and son of the railroad magnate John Murray Forbes.)

As America grew economically everyone, it seemed, wanted a stake. Even Captain Ahab. In Herman Melville's *Moby Dick*, the crew of the ill-fated *Pequod*, the ship condemned by Ahab to sail the world in search of a symbol, is also part of a capitalistic enterprise. In the whaling business, explains Ishmael, the book's narrator, no wages were paid to the seamen; but all hands, including the captain's, received "certain shares of the profits" called lays. Sounding more like something out of a shareholder's proxy statement, Ishmael continues: the lays "were proportioned to the degree of importance pertaining to the respective duties of the ship's company." Another character, Queequeg, a South Seas heathen, views the American voyage in a more universal manner: "It's a mutual, joint-stock world, in all meridians. We cannibals must help these Christians." Economically speaking, this is pure Adam Smith, who believed that although each individual was motivated by self-interest, each acted for the good of the whole, guided by the invisible hand of free competition. In a corporation with mutual shareholders pooling their capital, everyone is invested in everyone else to make things work.

As corporations sought capital for expansion, stock exchanges had organized in New York, Boston, and Philadelphia. Organized exchanges provided liquidity— active markets that traded stocks and bonds—for corporations in need of capital. By the 1850s, the stock market's lure had enticed small investors from every walk of life. They saw the market as a place where for a moderate risk they could get a return on their money without tying up their savings for long periods of time. Just before the panic of 1857, wrote James K. Medbery in *Wall Street*, "The entire country was in stocks. The farmer, the country lawyer, jobbers, heavy domestic dealers, the whole foreign trade, were more or less holders of shares, bonds, country, city, or state paper. These they used as capital, drew therefrom dividends or interest, raised money for immediate needs by hypothecation, and, in a word, based their business movements upon the belief that this property could always be converted into coin or employed as collaterals."

Such active markets became the stuff of fraud. "A game among plungers, 'Playing the Market' gave spice to drab mercantile existence, attracted little Daniels to the lions' den," observed Thomas Cochran and William Miller in *The Age of Enterprise*. "More important to the business community were the frauds perpetrated through the market." Much of the fraud involved the issuance of fake stocks. For instance, in 1854 Robert Schuyler, president of the New York and New

XYZ Company wants to raise money. If it's an established company it could sell off such assets as plants, office buildings, or land it may hold to raise cash. It also could sell one of its subsidiaries or divisions. But for a company that is either starting up or one that doesn't have extensive assets that can be sold to generate a big infusion of dollars, there are mainly two ways of raising capital: borrowing from a bank or some other financial institution like an insurance company. Or selling shares in XYZ to investors. The sale of new shares by the company takes place in the so-called primary market. But once shares are out in the market and are being bought and sold among investors, they are secondhand shares. And that secondhand market is called a secondary market. Trading existing shares in the secondary market does not raise new capital for the XYZ Company. Say the principal secondary marketplace for XYZ shares is the New York Stock Exchange (NYSE), where a buyer and seller are brought together through an intermediary known as a "specialist." Suppose you want to buy one hundred shares of XYZ. You contact a broker, who in turn relays the order to the floor of the NYSE. There the order goes to a specialist who keeps a record of the orders to buy and sell XYZ. He will look at your order to see if an investor is prepared to sell at the price you seek. Rather than match you up with an outside seller, the specialist has an alternative: He may be able to buy your stock from one of the other floor brokers who are gathered around, or he may sell you the stock from the inventory of shares he owns. However, if no one is ready to sell at your price, the specialist will make a note of your order and hold it, until he can execute it. The NYSE, which trades an average of 270 million shares a day in some three thousand companies, isn't the only stock market in the United States There are regional stock exchanges as well as the over-the-counter market, where stocks are traded through a network of dealers who use a system of computer terminals known as NASDAQ (National Association of Securities Dealers Automated Quotations System).

ABOVE: THE NEW YORK STOCK EXCHANGE BUILDING ON WALL STREET. THE FIRST MARKET IN THE U.S. WAS FORMED NEAR HERE IN 1792. COURTESY AMERICAN BANK NOTE COMPANY.

IT IS HEREBY Certified by the President and Managers of the

N.º 113 PENNSYLVANIA Population Company,

THAT *Theophilus Cazenove Esquire*

is entitled to one Share of Stock in the said Company, Numbered *One Hundred & Thirteen*

Transferable in the presence of the Treasurer by the said *Theophilus Cazenove* or *his* Attorney;

subject nevertheless to the payments due or payable thereupon, according to the Terms of the Plan of the Association.

Done in pursuance of an Order of the Board, and given under the Hand and Seal of the President, this *Fourth* day of *July* in the Year of our Lord One Thousand Seven Hundred and Ninety-*two*.

W. Nicholson, President.

Countersigned,

Treasurer.

Francis Bailey, Printer.

THE PENNSYLVANIA POPULATION COMPANY

ABOVE: THE PENNSYLVANIA POPULA-TION COMPANY (1792) IS ONE OF THE RAREST EARLY SHARES AND IS CONSIDERED ONE OF THE FIRST DOCUMENTED STOCK CERTIFICATES IN AMERICA. IT ALSO SET A PRECEDENT—ORNAMENTATION. THOUGH THE BORDERS ARE PRIMITIVE COMPARED TO LATER SPECIMENS, IT DISPLAYS AN AURA OF AUTHORITY AKIN TO A PROCLAMATION. THE SHARE WAS PRINTED BY FRANCES BAILEY AND SIGNED ON JULY 4. COURTESY OF RICHARD GREGG.

Haven Railroad, sold $2 million of unauthorized shares in his company. That same year Alexander Kyle, who headed the Harlem Railroad, issued some $300,000 of forged stock, and the officials of Parker Vein Coal Company sold five times as many shares as their charter authorized. And there was the scam of Edward Crane, president of Vermont Central Railroad, who sold ten thousand illegitimate shares, forcing the Vermont legislature to increase the authorized capitalization of his railroad to save his victims from being fleeced.

As commodities prices fell by 15 percent from the previous year, speculation on the New York Stock Exchange, the most liquid market in the country at the time, was rampant. Investors had been able to borrow freely from banks to finance their stock purchases, which fueled the speculative fever. When the Ohio Life Insurance & Trust Company failed in 1857, western banks began to demand their funds from New York. Banks had to call in loans forcing speculators to sell stocks at any price to raise cash. The chain reaction set off the panic of 1857. By year's end, stock prices on the NYSE dropped 45 percent, and failures included such railroad companies as the Reading, Erie, Illinois Central, and Michigan Central. Many banks—eighteen small and medium-sized ones in New York alone—had failed as well because they had depended on railroad securities for their own collateral. The 1857 collapse took its toll in other ways. Writes Robert Sobel in *Panic on Wall Street*: "On Wall Street it wiped out a generation of conservative, old-fashioned bankers and brokers, and made it possible for younger, more daring speculators to take their places." It also led to despair in the North and optimism in the South that cotton was king. In December 1857, *DeBow's Review* summed it up with a southern spin: "The wealth of the South is permanent and real, that of the North fugitive and fictitious.…" Four years later another panic would grab the nation, this one far costlier than any war between bulls and bears.

LEFT: PATRIOTS PROTESTED WHEN THE BRITISH IMPOSED THE STAMP ACT ON THE COLONIES IN 1765. ALMOST 100 YEARS LATER CAME A SIMILAR STAMP ACT, THIS TIME ENFORCED BY THE U.S. GOVERNMENT. PRESIDENT LINCOLN IMPOSED A TAX ON TRANSACTIONS INVOLVING STOCKS AND BONDS TO PAY FOR THE CIVIL WAR. THESE REVENUE STAMPS WERE IMPRINTED WITH GEORGE WASHINGTON'S IMAGE.

If you don't believe the world of collectibles is expanding, just call up e-Bay on your computer and peruse the mind-boggling prospects of a zillion items to buy and sell. Or tune into the popular PBS *Antiques Road Show,* where experts visit a new city every week to appraise thousands of flea-market finds. One relatively new collecting genre is called "scripophily," the collecting of canceled stocks and bonds.

Where does the term "scripophily" come from?

The word is half English and half Greek. "Scrip" is an ownership right, and "philos" means love. The word was coined in 1976 when the *Financial Times of London* sponsored a contest to name this hobby.

When did people begin to collect?

Initial interest on a large scale only began in the late 1970s in Switzerland and West Germany. It then took hold in England. Many of the European dealers began to buy in the United States. Since then interest has grown and there are now about two thousand collectors and some thirty dealers in the United States, a small group compared with, for example, coin or stamp collectors. There are perhaps seventy-five hundred collectors in the rest of the world, most of them in Western Europe.

Why collect?

There's value in old certificates because of their artwork and historical significance. Some dealers think of them as souvenirs of the American capitalist market. Others consider them antiques that document the building blocks of one of the greatest industrial powers in history.

What determines the value?

Supply and demand notwithstanding, a number of factors include: condition, age, historical relevance, signatures, rarity, demand for a particular security, aesthetics (the appearance based upon the vignette, color of ink, fancy borders, and calligraphy), type of company, original face value, bankers associated with issuance of the stock, transfer (tax) stamps, cancellation markings, type of engraving process, quality of paper, and whether the security was issued or unissued.

What's the difference between issued and unissued stock?

An unissued stock certificate was usually a printer's prototype stamped with the word "Specimen" on the face. Issued certificates, on the other hand, are those out in the marketplace, sold by the company that sought to raise capital from investors or shareholders. The issued certificates are considered to have more historical charm, which usually makes them more valuable and desirable. In some instances, however, issued certificates of a given type may no longer exist, and only the unissued certificate is available. In addition, an unissued share is often in better condition.

What is a cancellation?

The life of a stock certificate virtually has one holder. When the stock is sold the certificate must physically be canceled. When the stock is purchased, the investor receives a new certificate. The manner of cancellation can mean a great deal to the collector. Some are holed, cut, rubber-stamped, or pen-canceled with an "X" or line through the signatures or through the whole document. Some cancellations are unsightly; others detract very little.

Are all stocks canceled?

Yes. When a stock is sold, the certificate goes to the transfer agent, generally a bank or trust company appointed by the corporation to transfer its securities. The certificate is then stored for a period of time. After the time period expires, the Securities and Exchange Commission requires the transfer agent to destroy the certificate by sending it to a company that specializes in shredding securities. The destruction of certificates, thereby reducing the supply, could enhance the value of those in circulation. This is especially true today when more and more companies are issuing shares electronically as a so-called book entry to avoid the slow and cumbersome paperwork involved in issuing stock certificates. Some companies actually charge a fee if the investor demands the actual certificate.

Are certificates graded like coins and stamps?

Condition is an important factor and as prices have increased, specific descriptions and grading have become necessary. The grading standards for stocks and bonds widely followed are: UNC (uncirculated)—clean and crisp as issued; EF (extremely fine)—clean, but perhaps traces of folds, almost as issued; VF (very fine)—minor folds or creases, showing slight wear; F (fine)—very creased or worn, but still perfectly clear; and Fair—extremely creased and worn, an item that has been widely circulated.

Are the older pieces more valuable than the modern ones?

Generally, yes. Age, however, is not always a big factor. Graphics, supply, and popularity are considerations. More modern certificates dating from the 1950s to the 1980s are often available in large quantities and for this reason there are many certificates available in the one dollar to three dollar range. Consequently, a collection can be built on a modest budget. But experts advise collectors to specialize in a specific topic, like railroads or autos or pre–Civil War or mining issues or stocks from a certain region if your budget is limited.

What is the most valuable stock or bond?

In recent years the highest price paid for a stock certificate by an American collector was $33,000 for the Bank of North America, dated June 7, 1783, which is the nation's oldest surviving stock certificate. It's still a modest price compared with stamps or coins that have fetched a million dollars at auction. But it is a clear indication that values are climbing. For instance, in 1980 the highest price paid at auction for an American stock or bond was for the New York and Harlem Rail Road Company stock certificate. Signed by Commodore Vanderbilt, the certificate sold for $3,000. Recently the New York and Harlem stock sold for $12,000. Over the same period, an American Express Company certificate (from the 1850s) increased in price from $500 to $3,500. In early 1980 a Standard Oil of Ohio (circa 1875–1882) certificate sold for $150. Today it's worth between $8,000 and $15,000.

Why are autographed stocks and bonds so valuable?

Celebrity has always carried a price tag. And it's no different in the business world. The financial and economic growth of the United States was often in the hands of such men as the Vanderbilts, Astors, Carnegies, Fords, Rockefellers, and Goulds. Autographed pieces are the gems of the field because of their rarity and the strong demand. Thus they command premium prices. One of the most highly valued certificates currently around is that of Buffalo Bill's Wild West Company signed by William F. Cody (Buffalo Bill).

DOES GEOGRAPHICAL LOCATION HAVE ANYTHING TO DO WITH VALUE?

Yes. A particular state, town, or region of the country may be important to one collector and not to another. Western stocks and bonds are generally quite scarce and in strong demand. The securities of some southern states are also scarce and sell at premium prices.

DOES IT MATTER WHO THE PRINTER IS?

Yes, but only because some printers have been particularly known for consistently fine quality. The American Bank Note Company is the best known for excellent work. The New York Stock Exchange requires that the name of the engraving company appear upon the face of all its listed stocks and also upon the face of coupons and title panel of each bond. (Other elements on the face of a stock certificate include a registration number assigned by the SEC to thwart the sale of stolen certificates; the number of shares, the stock's par value, an arbitrary value assigned to the stock; the name of the issuer; the corporate seal; and an identification number issued by the Committee on Uniform Securities Identification Procedures [CUSIP] to improve the efficiency of clearing operations).

DO COLORS MEAN ANYTHING?

Both color and artwork are extremely important. A red, green, gold, and black bond will generally look more impressive than a plain black bond. Reds and blues are desirable, but the color preference is often a matter of a collector's personal taste, just as with the vignette (the small engraved picture) on the face of the certificate. Modern four-color certificates are very popular because they are uncommon.

WHAT IS THE MOST POPULAR TYPE OF STOCK TO COLLECT?

Railroad stocks and bonds are by far the most actively collected, with mining in second place. According to dealer estimates, there are at least two hundred thousand varieties of railroad and bond certificates. Incidentally, a bond coupon detached from the bond carries no value.

ARE AUCTION PRICES REALISTIC GUIDES OR DO THEY REFLECT TRUE VALUE?

No. True value is what one person is willing to pay for an item. In auctions, this rule may apply to a point. Still, the passions and apathy of the bidders present can affect the realized price.

AS IN THE ART WORLD, ARE THERE REPRODUCTIONS AND FAKE STOCK CERTIFICATES?

Yes, but they are rare. So far they have not bothered dealers or collectors. Still, as the field grows, it is likely forgeries will appear.

OPPOSITE: THE KENTUCKY AND GREAT EASTERN RAILWAY CONNECTED THE COAL AND IRON MINES OF EASTERN KENTUCKY AND WEST VIRGINIA WITH CINCINNATI, OHIO. COLLECTORS BELIEVE IT IS PIONEER DANIEL BOONE PICTURED IN THE TOP VIGNETTE OF THIS 1872 BOND. COURTESY OF GEORGE LABARRE.

UNITED STATES OF AMERICA

KENTUCKY AND GREAT EASTERN

Chartered under the Laws of the — Commonwealth of Kentucky.

ORGANIZED — JUNE 1871.

Nº 1366 — Nº 1366

1000 — **1000**

GOLD — RAILWAY COMPANY — BOND

BEARING 7 PER CENT GOLD INTEREST, FREE OF U.S. TAXES.

Promises to pay to the holder of this Bond Twenty years after date for value received at the Agency of the Company in the City of New York **ONE THOUSAND DOLLARS** in United States Gold Coin and also interest thereon at the rate of Seven per cent per annum payable semi-annually in Gold Coin free of United States taxes, upon the presentation of the annexed interest Coupons at the said Agency in the City of New York.

This Bond with others for the aggregate sum of Two millions, one hundred and ninety thousand dollars is secured by a first mortgage dated the 15th day of February A.D. 1872, conveying in Trust to the Farmers Loan and Trust Company of New York. All the right, title, interest and property which the said Railway Company has or may at any time hereafter acquire in or of the Railway above named from the City of Newport Campbell County, Kentucky upon along or near the Southern bank of the Ohio River, within said State of Kentucky to a point on the State line between the States of Kentucky and West Virginia at or near Catlettsburg, Boyd County, Kentucky a distance of One hundred and forty six miles be the same more or less and all its equipments property, corporate franchises and appendages of every nature as in said mortgage set forth.

This Bond is exchangeable at the option of the holder for a Registered Bond of like tenor and date on presentation at the office of the Company. In testimony whereof the said Company has caused these presents to be executed by its President and Secretary and its corporate seal to be affixed at Cincinnati Ohio this 15th day of February A.D. 1872.

_____ Secretary — _____ President

We hereby Certify that the Kentucky and Great Eastern Railway Company by to the Farmers Loan and Trust Company of New York in Trust to secure the in mentioned and described to wit. The entire Railway which the said Company and franchises of the said Company, and all its property real and personal in possession and the same. We further Certify that the said mortgage has been duly executed and delivered is filed and recorded in the proper offices in the State of Kentucky according to law for the exclu- to be issued to an amount not exceeding fifteen thousand Dollars per mile of the said mentioned and described.

mortgage dated the 15th day of February A.D. 1872 has granted and conveyed payment of certain Coupon Bonds of which this is one the following property there- has undertaken to construct under its charter together with the rights privileges which may be acquired, and all the right, title and interest of the said Company of in and to to us and the necessary amount of Internal Revenue Stamps affixed thereon and cancelled, and give benefit and security of the holders of this and other Bonds of said Company issued and Railway and franchises, and is the first and only mortgage on the property therein

The Mortgage by which this Bond is secured is duly stamped.

_____ Register — _____ Trustee

American Bank Note Co. N.Y. & Cin'ti

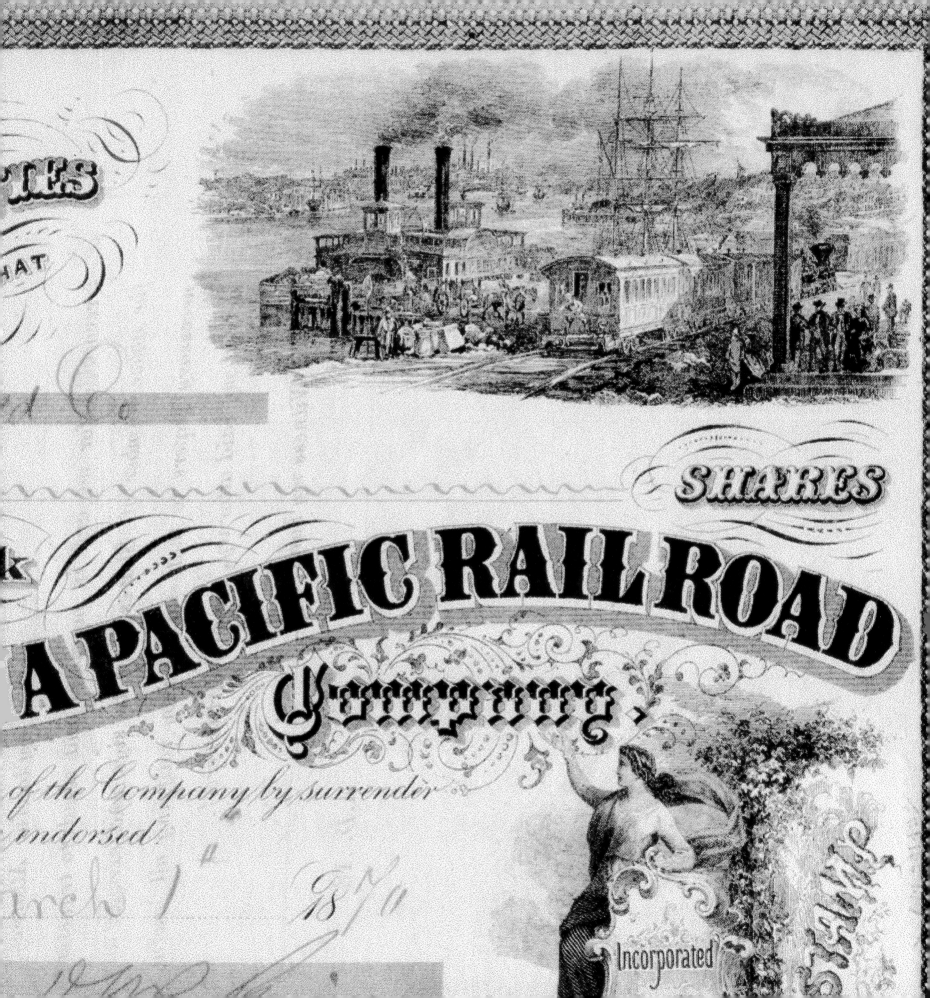

SHARES

A PACIFIC RAILROAD *Company*

of the Company by surrender

endorsed

March 1 *18* *70*

Incorporated

The sense of a national economic mutuality blew apart on April 12, 1861, when the sound of cannons thundered for the first time in the United States in fifty years, marking the start of the Civil War. The North had the railroads, arms makers, financiers, and men. By comparison, the South, as historians Thomas Cochran and William Miller, summed it up, "had nothing—except generals." At the outbreak of the Civil War, even the New York Stock Exchange suspended trading in seceding states. The war had started during a depression and few industries rallied throughout its duration.

AN INDUSTRIAL NATION

Shipping plummeted, railroad building came to a virtual halt, and textile producers couldn't get raw materials. The southern debt mounted, disrupting northern credit lines. In the North there were consolidations: The New York Central Railroad tried to merge with the Harlem, the Hudson River, and the Lake Shore Railroads. There were mergers in the salt and paper industries as John D. Rockefeller began to collect oil refineries, combining five of them during the war. By 1865, Western Union had acquired or built some fifty thousand miles of line, twice as much as its two rivals combined.

The Civil War that split a nation—costing 620,000 American lives—acted as a catalyst to push many industries out of the Middle Ages. The stock exchange, which had closed for a week in 1865 following the assassination of President Lincoln, began to flourish, boosted by factories and railroads in the North that had built the Union war machine, as well as the emergence of the "modern" corporation and its need for an amount of capital no individual could muster alone. In 1863, the New York Stock & Exchange Board changed its name to the New York Stock Exchange, and two years later it moved into its permanent home on Broad Street, just south of Wall Street. America stood on the brink of prospering and Americans, at least those who were inured to risk, loved the appeal of common stocks, which in the decades after the Civil War helped Cornelius

OPPOSITE: THE CALIFORNIA PACIFIC WAS THE LITTLE RAILROAD THAT COULD, THOUGH ITS MAIN LINE COVERED JUST 141 MILES. THE VIGNETTE DISPLAYS THE FACETS OF ITS OPERATIONS: RAILROAD SERVICE, STEAMSHIP LINE, AND CARGO HAULING. COURTESY OF DAVID M. BEACH.

Vanderbilt unify his railroads, J. P. Morgan fund his mergers, and Jay Gould play the market for fun and profit. From across the nation, millions of dollars flowed into New York, strengthening its position, concluded Cochran and Miller, "as the real capital of the nation."

That's not to say the road to economic recovery in the post–Civil War years was without its stomach-churning dips. Two-thirds of the years between 1837 and 1894 were marked by panics—the bottoms of economic cycles—that would be called depressions or recessions in modern times. Throughout 1873 banks and businesses across the nation fell like dominoes, pushed over the brink by financial panic that froze commerce in most American cities. On the streets of Chicago some people died of hunger. Others without jobs and homes huddled on the first floor of City Hall. Still others took to the streets, waving protest signs declaring "Bread or blood!" through the frigid air. Remarkably no shots were fired in this incident, which became known as the Bread Riot. The panic of 1873 claimed legions of investors, bud-

ding entrepreneurs, and economic titans. Big railroads and eastern financial firms went belly-up, closing the New York Stock Exchange for ten days. The entire banking system imploded like a black hole, sucking down twenty-two thousand businesses and millions of depositors.

Among the bankrupt casualties were the Northern Pacific Railroad, the Union Trust Company, the National Bank of the Commonwealth, and Jay Cook & Company, one of the nation's major financiers during the Civil War. Eventually, global depression swept across the oceans, and five hundred thousand Americans became unemployed with no safety net. But the United States and the rest of the world scrambled back to solvency just as they had from panic attacks in 1819, 1837, 1854, and 1857.

During the long peace that followed the Civil War, however, individual American wealth grew rapidly. America's

ABOVE, LEFT: PORTRAIT OF JAY GOULD. COURTESY OF AMERICAN BANK NOTE COMPANY. ABOVE: THE ERIE RAILROAD COMPANY, INCORPORATED IN 1832, OPERATED 2,300 MILES OF TRACK ACROSS NEW YORK STATE AND WENT BANKRUPT FOUR TIMES IN ITS HISTORY. THE RAILROAD PASS SHOWN ABOVE BEARS THE SIGNATURE OF JAY GOULD. COURTESY OF R.M. SMYTHE & CO., INC.

STATE OF OHIO.

Niles & New Lisbon Railway Co.

CHARTERED APRIL 1869. PERPETUAL.

SHARES $50 EACH.

I hereby Certify that James Fisk Jr. Trustee is entitled to Six Hundred and Sixty two Shares of the Capital Stock of the NILES AND NEW LISBON RAILWAY COMPANY, transferable only on the Books of the said Company by the said stockholder or his representative or Attorney on the surrender of this Certificate.

Dated at Niles this 31st day of December 1870

Sect.   Pres!

NILES AND NEW LISBON RAILWAY COMPANY

ABOVE: This tiny railroad, which operated for just 38 miles between Niles and Lisbon, Ohio, was typical of the local transportation railroads of the nineteenth century. Two members of its seven-man board were the notorious, yet soft-spoken Jay Gould, and the boisterous Jim Fisk, who treated Wall Street like an untamed frontier when they tried to corner the nation's gold market in 1869 and wrestled control of the Erie Railway away from chairman Daniel Drew and his rival Cornelius Vanderbilt. Courtesy of David M. Beach.

PULLMAN'S PALACE CAR COMPANY

ABOVE AND OPPOSITE: This stock certificate bears the signatures of a pair of America's greatest industrialists—Andrew Carnegie's on the reverse side and George Pullman's on the face. Pullman founded the company in 1876 after public acceptance of his "Pioneer" sleeping car, which revolutionized long-distance railroad travel. No longer did passengers have to sleep sitting up in their seats or stay in the usually inferior trackside hotels. Guided by his business acumen, Pullman's Palace Car Company grew to become the world's greatest maker of railroad cars.

KNOW ALL MEN BY THESE PRESENTS

That I Andrew Carnegie of N.Y.
do truly appoint Chs W Powell to be my
true and lawful Attorney to sell and transfer to Geo Lauder
Thirty (30) of the within named Shares
of the Capital Stock of PULLMAN'S PALACE CAR COMPANY with power to nominate
one or more persons under _____ and to do all necessary acts to accomplish that purpose.
Dated at N.Y. March 29th 187 5.
signed A Carnegie L.S.

G.F. McCandless

hereby nominate _____
substitute with all the powers above conferred on me
Dated _____ 187
signed _____ L.S.

exclusive club of millionaires had swelled to 3,800 by 1900, when one-tenth of the population owned nine-tenths of the wealth. The reign of agrarianism was replaced by a kingdom of tough-minded businessmen, trusts, corporations, and Washington railroad lobbyists—all calculating to accumulate capital. In the scramble, hardly anyone minded that seven out of ten industrial workers were earning no more than ten cents an hour or that children under fifteen were sweating in coal mines, steel mills, and tobacco fields for as little as twenty-five cents a day.

Even those of the upper middle class didn't mind working ten hours a day, six days a week. "The husbands are content to slave in business in order that their wives and families may live in ease and affluence," observed two visiting Englishmen in their *Reminiscences of America*, published in the early 1870s when the Victorians with their garish tastes and tasteless palates had taken over the parlors of America, filling them with wicker rockers, lamps, pianos, and countless knickknacks. In the eyes of artist Everett Shinn, American tastes during the Gilded Age were "swaddled in accessories fenced in with tasseled ropes and weighted down with chatelaines of bronze name plates."

Those flamboyant tastes were catered to by the designers and engravers of bank notes and stock certificates as early as the 1830s. To sell allegorical representation with its ornate intaglio swirls was to sell refinement to an emerging middle class. "In this sense the classical taste in America was profoundly democratic," notes Richard Bushman in the introduction to *Classical Tastes in America*. "From this time on, every stylistic change at the upper levels of society took popular forms that were disseminated among the middle class." The need to identify with classical cultures, Bushman continues, made the architects and their patrons embrace "the pillars and porticoes of the ancient world as if they were natural parents." The classical Grecian and Roman images proliferated: on bridges, bathhouses, pumping stations, water works, banks, courthouses, asylums, and even on cemetery entrances.

The architects of the period already realized that the classical connoted solidity and designed buildings to look like Roman temples. Among them were the Virginia state capitol, designed by Thomas Jefferson, Latrobe's Bank of Pennsylvania, William Strickland's Second Bank of the United States, and Thomas Walter's Founders Hall at Girad College. Thirty years later, the architect John Kellum would design the first permanent home of the New York Stock Exchange in classical Roman style, too.

OPPOSITE: STOCK VIGNETTES USED IN CERTIFICATES FOR SCIENCE AND RESEARCH (TOP) AND MINING AND MANUFACTURING (BOTTOM). BOTH, COURTESY OF AMERICAN BANK NOTE.

The new wave of classicism gave artist-engravers like Asher Durand, who knew neither Greek nor Latin, a chance to dabble in classical symbolism. Durand was the first to popularize gods and goddesses in vignettes on currency, bonds, and stocks. He gave Archimedes, Neptune, and Hercules local meaning by showing them interacting with American cogwheels, canal locks, cargo boats, trains, cows, and mountains. Nearly a century before a nude appeared on the Playboy

BUFFALO, BRADFORD AND PITTSBURGH RAIL ROAD COMPANY

ABOVE: THE BUFFALO, BRADFORD AND PITTSBURGH RAILROAD COMPANY SHARE (1869) IS ONE OF THREE KNOWN STOCK CERTIFICATES SIGNED BY JAY GOULD. THE RAILROAD BARON, AN INFAMOUS SWINDLER, MADE HIS INITIAL FORTUNE BY WATERING DOWN THE STOCK OF THE ERIE LINE IN NEW YORK. THE CAPER IS SAID TO HAVE NET HIM $64 MILLION. COURTESY OF GEORGE HEWITSON COLLECTIBLES.

Enterprises certificate, Durand made the nude on a stock certificate fashionable. He revealed the classic-style female body, sometimes even naked above the waist. In its day, such public rendering was sensational with all the shock value of *Playboy* magazine when it first hit the newsstands in 1953.

"Without Asher Durand, certificates of companies formed in the 1890s might carry pictures of ladies in bustles, and those of companies in the 1920s might be perpetuating the shapeless styles of that decade," wrote William Griffiths in his *History of American Bank Note Company*. Asher's older brother, Cyrus, was the technical genius who worked at American Bank Note for a number of years. Both brothers had learned their trade under Peter Maverick, New York's first engraver, before they joined forces with a business colleague in 1824 and opened A.B.& C. Durand & Co. in New York.

Soon they were busy commodifying and disseminating classicism. They offered specimen sheets that demonstrated the wide variety of designs and vignettes available to customers. The idea that one could buy vignettes piecemeal to customize a bank note, bond, or stock certificate was a perfect fit for the times. In essence the Durands were offering a designer certificate, a trendy object for an aspiring class that sought upward mobility. Buying a stake in a company whose share certificate oozed classical glory and virtue was now fashionably refined.

A look at a Durand specimen sheet reveals: Neptune drawn by prancing horses, with a ship under full sail in the background; Archimedes on a cloud lifting the world with a lever, its fulcrum, supposedly an American mountain peak with a canal lock at its base; a female figure in a flowing garment representing Justice, a sword in one hand and a pair of scales in the other, with a bust of Washington on a pedestal behind her; Franklin, seated on a chair, in relief against clouds streaked with lightning, and at his feet an open book titled *Franklin's Works: Mind Your Business*; a graceful semi-clad female figure holding a flagon and cup, quenching the thirst of the American eagle; another female figure holding a torch that illuminates the globe; Hercules slaying the Hydra.

Banks loved Durand's style and ordered all kinds of fancy and elegant designs for their bank notes. New York's Chemical Bank, for example, ordered a plate with a portrait of Martin Van Buren, then U.S. president, together with the

ABOVE: BY 1893—THE YEAR NASSAU ELECTRIC RAILROAD WAS INCORPORATED—ELECTRICITY WAS ARCING IN HOMES AND OFFICES THROUGH THE INCANDESCENT BULBS, ALTERNATING CURRENT WAS PUSHING POWER TRANSMISSIONS OVER LONG DISTANCES, AND ELECTRIC TRACTION SYSTEMS WERE IN COMMERCIAL USE IN A DOZEN AMERICAN CITIES. COURTESY DAVID M. BEACH.

CAPITAL
1.600.000
DOLLARS

1600 SHARES
$ 1000 EACH

Bella V

THIS CERTIFIE

BELLA U

Transferable

BELLA UNION GOLD & SILVER MINING COMPANY

ABOVE AND OPPOSITE: BELLA UNION WAS AMONG THE THOUSANDS OF MINING COMPANIES THAT DOTTED THE WEST IN THE WAKE OF THE 1849 CALIFORNIA GOLD RUSH. AS WITH RAILROADS AND FINANCE, MINING ALSO HAD ITS MOGULS. AMONG THEM WERE THE BIG FOUR— JAMES HAGGIN, MARCUS DALY, AND LLOYD AND GEORGE HEARST. GEORGE WAS THE PRESIDENT OF BELLA UNION AND FATHER OF WILLIAM RANDOLPH HEARST, WHO WOULD CARVE OUT HIS OWN DYNASTY IN THE NEWSPAPER WORLD. THROUGH THEIR SYNDICATE, THE BIG FOUR OWNED OR CONTROLLED ONE HUNDRED GOLD, SILVER, AND COPPER MINES. COURTESY DAVID M. BEACH.

figure of a chemist in a laboratory, both for the margin of a bank note, with an eagle for the vignette.

Popularizing images in this way, Durand had turned the faces of the bank note and the stock certificate into something they had never been before: art that was nostalgic, provocative, exhibitionist, even erotic for the times. And to buy such art from a specimen sheet was like buying a new car and choosing the model and color that made it seem unique.

The Durands were typical of America's young artisans who had flocked to engravers' workshops since the early colonial days, asking to do original work. Many did so because engravers were the most prosperous of American artists with jobs galore for beginners who wanted to learn a trade. One of the first was Paul Revere, a silversmith by trade, who added engraving to his artistic endeavors in 1770 when he produced a hymn book, *The New England Psalm Singer*. In the following years he engraved pictures on political subjects and designed and engraved the seal of Phillips Academy in Andover. By 1775, Revere became a bank-note engraver. And since he was the first bank-note engraver in *independent* America, some historians consider him the father of the industry in the United States. America's first bank-note engraver, however, preceded Revere by more than seventy years at a time when banks and colonies were issuing their own private currencies in the form of bank notes and so-called bills of credit. In 1702, Jno Conny (the name as it appears on a billing statement) engraved three bills of credit for the Massachusetts colonial government. Durand's reputation was established in 1820 with his engraving of John

Trumbull's famous painting, *Declaration of Independence.* Other noted artists who were either engravers, etchers, or designers included Edwin Blashfiled and Alonzo Foringer, both muralists, James D. Smillie, and Winslow Homer—one of America's most influential late nineteenth century painters—who etched vignettes on stone for Boston lithographer John H. Bufford. Bufford's imprint is found on stock certificates such as Main Central Rail Road Company.

As America developed, so did the industry for creating and designing bank notes and stock certificates—primarily as an effort to thwart counterfeiting, a crime as old as recorded history. So the union of commerce and art became a marriage of convenience as Americans pushed westward farther from the big banks in the east.

In the years ahead, Cyrus Durand, a tinkerer by nature, would invent an array of engraving tools to enhance designs. They included machines for engraving straight lines, wavy lines, and ovals; a pantograph size-reducing machine; and a transferring machine. After President Andrew Jackson closed the Bank of the United States as a populist gesture, local banks resumed issuing their own paper currencies. The bills, designed and printed in engraving shops, became a counterfeiter's delight. The banks turned to Cyrus who invented a geometric lathe, which ruled lines on the plate that no counterfeiter could match. After spending the first two decades of his working life as an engraver, in 1832 Cyrus's brother, Asher turned to painting portraits, and then, encouraged by Thomas Cole, a leading landscape painter, he established himself as one of the premier artists of the Hudson River School.

NEW-ORLEANS, JACKSON & GREAT NORTHERN RAILROAD COMPANY

ABOVE: EVER WONDER WHAT RETIRED CONFEDERATE GENERALS DID AFTER THE CIVIL WAR? MANY OF THEM TURNED IN THEIR SABERS AND SADDLES FOR A PEN AND DESK TO BECOME BUSINESSMEN. GENERAL PIERRE GUSTAVE TOUTANT BEAUREGARD, WHO COMMANDED THE BOMBARDMENT OF FORT SUMTER THAT BEGAN THE CIVIL WAR, BECAME PRESIDENT OF THE NEW-ORLEANS JACKSON, A SMALL RAIL LINE WITH JUST 206 MILES OF TRACK THAT RAN BETWEEN NEW ORLEANS AND CANTON, MISSISSIPPI. FROM 1870 TO 1888, HE WAS MANAGER OF THE LOUISIANA LOTTERY. COURTESY OF DAVID M. BEACH.

Dr. Seth Hudson, a native of Lexington, Massachusetts, was one of America's earliest men of confidence who successfully parted a fool and his money. A forger of provincial bank notes, Hudson and his confederate, John Howe, were caught and convicted in 1762. The sentence: Hudson was pilloried and Howe whipped. Hudson moved on to Hoosuck, Massachusetts, now Williamstown, where he promptly pulled his scam on the townsfolk there. No one seems to know his fate, but Hudson is an early reminder that money has never been safe from the mischief of the counterfeiter.

In the land of free enterprise, Hudson's misfortune was another man's opportunity. While Hudson was in the pillory, Nathaniel Hurd, America's first engraver, was literally sketching him in his misery.

Chances are Hudson would have been long forgotten had not Hurd engraved his drawings of Hudson and Howe being punished and then sold the prints. (Financially, Hudson probably would have been better off cutting a deal with Hurd for a percentage on each print that he sold.) In 1760, Hurd advertised his services in the *Boston Gazette* as an engraver of many metals, including gold, silver, copper, brass, and steel.

Meanwhile, super-patriot Paul Revere was making his mark as a premier engraver. Though his midnight ride from Charlestown to Lexington in April 1775 to warn of the approaching British troops may have been his most famous exploit, Revere was also known for his work as a silversmith and engraver. When the rebels issued the first security to finance the Revolutionary War they turned to

ABOVE: AMERICAN BANK NOTE COMPANY'S HEADQUARTERS BUILDING AT 70 BROAD STREET IN NEW YORK CITY, ERECTED IN 1908. COURTESY AMERICAN BANK NOTE. OPPOSITE: CHICAGO AND ALTON RAILROAD COMPANY BOND CIRCA 1899. COURTESY DAVID M. BEACH.

Paul Revere, who engraved the so-called King Philip Bond. For the Massachusetts colony he also produced a series of bank notes that bore a picture of a man holding a sword that became known as "sword hand money." A decade earlier, Benjamin Franklin had printed a threepence bank note for colonial Pennsylvania. Other colonies issued their own notes, including Rhode Island, New Hampshire, South Carolina, Georgia, and Connecticut.

Following the Revolutionary War, the first engraved bank notes to be circulated by a nongovernmental entity were those issued by the Bank of North America, which was authorized by the Continental Congress in 1781. The bank notes included a vignette by Charles Heath, at the time a prominent copperplate engraver of book and magazine illustrations. Three years later, the Bank of New York and the Bank of Massachusetts were formed. By 1791, the federally chartered Bank of the United States opened with its main office in Philadelphia where the nation's first mint was set up. Robert Scot was appointed its first engraver.

In succeeding years he was aided by Jacob Perkins, the Yankee inventor who advanced the art of engraving by devising a

UNITED STATES OF AMERICA

THE
CHICAGO AND ALTON
RAILROAD COMPANY.

N?
30026

N?
30026.

$1000.

$1000.

Three Per Cent. Refunding Fifty-Year Gold Bond,
DUE 1949.

The Chicago and Alton Railroad Company (hereinafter called the "Railroad Company"), for value received, hereby promises to pay to the bearer, or, if registered, to the registered holder of this bond, **One Thousand Dollars** in gold coin of the United States of America of or equal to the present standard of weight and fineness, on the first day of October in the year 1949, at the city of New York, and to pay interest thereon from October 1, 1899, at the rate of three per cent. per annum, payable in said city in like gold coin, semi-annually, on the first days of April and October in each year, upon presentation and surrender, as they severally mature, of the interest coupons hereto annexed. Both the principal and interest of this bond are payable without deduction for any tax or taxes which the Railroad Company may be required to pay or retain therefrom under any present or future law of the United States of America, or of any State, county or municipality therein.

This bond is one of a series of coupon bonds and registered bonds of the Railroad Company, known as its "Refunding Fifty-Year Gold Bonds," and which are to be issued to an amount not exceeding in the aggregate the principal sum of $40,000,000 at any one time outstanding, except as hereinafter mentioned, all of which bonds are issued and to be issued under and equally secured by a mortgage and deed of trust dated October 1st, 1899, executed by The Chicago and Alton Railroad Company to the Illinois Trust and Savings Bank, as Trustee, to which mortgage and deed of trust reference is made for a description of the properties and franchises mortgaged, the nature and extent of the security, the rights of the holders of bonds under the same, and the terms and conditions upon which the bonds are issued and secured. Power is reserved in said mortgage and deed of trust to issue additional bonds as therein specifically provided. This bond shall pass by delivery unless registered in the name of the owner on the books of the Railroad Company, such registry being noted on the bond by the Railroad Company. After such registry no transfer shall be valid unless made on said books by the registered holder in person or by his attorney duly authorized, and similarly noted on the bond, but the same may be discharged from registry by being transferred to bearer, and thereupon

CHICAGO AND ALTON RAILROAD COMPANY BOND, BACK DETAIL

ABOVE: THE CHICAGO AND ALTON WAS A WORKHORSE OF A RAILROAD, BUT IT IS MOST COMMONLY REMEMBERED FOR AN EVENT THAT ITS STOCK AND BOND HOLDERS WOULD HAVE LIKED TO FORGET: IT WAS THE LAST TRAIN TO BE ROBBED BY JESSE JAMES. ON SEPTEMBER 7, 1881, TWO MILES WEST OF GLENDALE, MISSOURI, THE JAMES-YOUNGER GANG HELD UP THE CHICAGO AND ALTON. AND THE EIGHT-MAN GANG ESCAPED WITH $15,000. COURTESY OF DAVID M. BEACH.

way to harden steel, which is far more durable than copper, for use in printing plates.

Engraving is the art of cutting lines on plates, blocks, or other shapes of metal, wood, or other material. There are four basic types of printing methods: relief, intaglio, planographic, and stencil. In the relief process, the print is made from the surface that remains in relief after areas of the block have been cut away. A sheet pressed down touches only the elevated surface. Originally known as cameo printing, its more popular name is letterpress. In the intaglio process, the print is made from the lines that are cut or etched below the surface of the plate. The process differs from that of printing from a wood block or other surface cut in relief. Instead of depositing ink on the raised surfaces, the printer fills the lines with ink and wipes the surface clean. The paper is then forced against the plate. In the planographic process, the print is made from a flat surface on which the printing and non-printing areas are practically at the same level. Known as surface printing, or lithography, the process is made possible by the principle that oil and water do not mix. The ink image of the plate is ink-receptive and refuses water and the non-image area is water-receptive and refuses ink. In the stencil

process, the print is made through openings or perforations in a stencil or screen.

The easiest line to engrave is a perfectly straight one. Curved lines demand greater skill and those with a curl require technical virtuosity. The commonly used plates for intaglio printing were either copper or steel. The softness of copper allowed it to be cut more easily, but the hardness of steel enabled a greater number of prints to be made from a plate. Until the early 1800s, copper had been the primary medium for engraving. Steel intaglio engraving is considered to be extremely difficult for the counterfeiter to imitate.

In 1810, Scot formed the nucleus of what would later become the American Bank Note Company. With three other engravers he formed Murray, Draper, Fairman & Co. The firm hired Asa Spencer, who improved the geometric lathe, a machine invented by French watchmakers. The lathe slowly rotated a piece of steel in complicated patterns while a stationery graving tool sank a line into its surface. The result were swirls that could not be reproduced unless one knew how to fix the settings of the machine, and they were too precise to be copied freehand. The border of every stock certificate, bond, bank note, and traveler's check in use today is created by the geometric lathe.

Spencer, who died in 1847, was succeeded by Cyrus Durand, whose older brother, Asher, would become the first engraver to popularize Greek gods and goddesses on vignettes of bank notes, bonds, and stock certificates. But it was Cyrus, the technical genius, who improved many of the engraving tools, including machines for engraving wavy lines, straight lines, and ovals, and a pantograph size-reducing machine. Without the benefit of Perkins's secret design for mechanically duplicating an engraved steel die—a process known as transferring—Durand made a transferring machine as well as a geometric lathe.

In 1858, seven engraving firms merged to form the Association of American Bank Note Company (ABNCo.) The firms included Danforth, Perkins & Co.; Toppan, Carpenter & Co.; Draper, Welsh & Co.; Bald, Cousland & Co.; Rawdon, Wright, Hatch & Edson; John E. Gavit; and Wellstood, Hay & Whiting. The newly formed company was well received by the banks and companies that were its clients because it promised the stability, security, and continuity that users of bank notes, stock certificates, and bonds had long desired. Rawdon, Wright, Hatch & Edson was the largest of these firms and produced the first U.S. postage stamps. The firm also established the use of green as the traditional color of money, again as a means to foil counterfeiters.

During the Civil War the United States monetary system was radically altered with the passage of the National Bank Act that gave the federal government sole control over the issuance of bank notes. American Bank Note Company won a portion of the business of printing the new U.S. currency, turning out millions of bank notes annually, plus postage stamps and securities certificates for public and private users. The company also expanded internationally, printing currencies, bonds, and stamps for Argentina, Brazil, Columbia, Ecuador, Greece, Italy, Peru, and Uruguay.

Throughout the post–Civil War period, with the rapid rise of the railroads that created demand for stocks and bonds, American Bank Note Company thrived in the private sector as well. In 1874, in an effort to make stock certificates more secure against counterfeiters, the New York Stock Exchange issued rules that every company listed on the exchange have "carefully engraved certificates by some responsible Bank Note Company." In subsequent years the NYSE amplified the original rule to require, among other elements, a vignette on the face of a security, a colored border, and the descriptive or promissory portion of the document printed in black or in black combined with a color.

In 1875, the Treasury Department's Bureau of Engraving and Printing was set up to print all U.S. bank notes and securities. It cost American Bank Note Company a huge portion of its business. The company, on the ropes, was forced to consolidate its operations with those of another financial engraver to end the crisis. The new company prospered in the 1880s and the 1890s, however, riding the boom of America's industrial expansion, much of it publicly financed with stocks and bonds. Moreover, the company prospered into the twentieth century from the growing number of foreign governments using American Bank Note Company currency notes.

Two innovations came in 1891. The first was American Bank Note Company's introduction of "planchette paper," which contained colored paper discs rather than silk fibers or silk threads. Supplied by Crane & Co., the discs have various characteristics that reveal any counterfeit. The second innovation was introduced by one of the company's long-standing customers, the American Express Company. The new product was the traveler's check. Today American Bank Note Company supplies virtually all of the major U.S. banks with these forms.

Into the twentieth century American Bank Note Company continued to acquire other engravers, whose business was mainly securities printing. Among the acquisitions were such firms as Franklin, Homer Lee, Western, and International. In 1990, U.S. Bank Note Corporation merged with American Bank Note. Currently ABN is one of three companies that comprise United States Banknote Corporation, a holding company whose stock trades on the NYSE. The other two affiliated businesses are American Banknote Company Grafica e Servicos Ltd, the largest private sector security printer in Brazil; and American Bank Note Holographics, Inc., the world's largest producer of holograms—images made by lasers—for security applications.

By 1999, two centuries after Robert Scot founded ABN's bank note business, the world of money and investment has grown to unimaginable dimensions. Currently economists estimate there are $480 billion of U.S. currency in the country and abroad (that's nearly $1,800 for every child and adult in America). No one has come up with a total value of all the stocks, bonds, and other securities held throughout the world. But one thing is for sure, the battle continues to make them safe from the scheme of the counterfeiter.

All along, the key to a thriving economy was transportation whether it was moving people or cattle from one place to another. The opening of the Erie Canal in 1825 had spurred migration westward, helping to transform sleepy, mud-drenched hamlets into rapidly growing towns. The opening of the Erie Canal made New York City the seaboard gateway for the Great Lakes region. New York State bonds issued to finance the canal began trading on the New York Stock Exchange. Eventually, Chicago became the junction of America's two great inland waterways. The water route for commerce stretched westward from the Erie Canal through the Great Lakes to the Chicago River, then through the Illinois and Michigan Canal and down the Mississippi, to the thriving ports of St. Louis and New Orleans. But travel was still relatively slow.

WESTWARD HO

In 1840, from New York via rivers, canals, and turnpikes it took nearly a week to reach Cleveland or Louisville, two weeks to St. Louis or New Orleans, and three weeks to Chicago and Milwaukee. The railroad, promoters insisted, would change movement dramatically. And those communities who realized this took an economic leap over others. For instance, Congress authorized construction of the Illinois and Michigan Canal in 1836, just three years after Chicago was incorporated. That year Illinois built its first railway, the Galena and Chicago Union Railroad, when there was barely a thousand miles of track in all of America. The rail link connected Chicago with the Mississippi barge trade and the grain fields in the northwestern part of Illinois.

At the same time, immigrants—many arriving by railway—poured into cities and towns with Old World perseverance, a willingness to sweat, and a certain naivete that came with unfettered optimism. They began replacing American labor in railroad and canal construction work, in packing plants, stockyards, and shoe factories. In 1850, there were more immigrants in St. Louis and Chicago than natives. By the late 1880s, immigrants—arriving on American shores from Europe at the

OPPOSITE: IN THE LATE NINETEENTH CENTURY, RAILROADS WERE A GAME OF SURVIVAL. CHICAGO AND EASTERN'S ROOTS GREW FROM THE FORECLOSURE OF THE CHICAGO, DANVILLE, AND VINCENNES RAIL ROAD COMPANY. COURTESY OF KEN PRAG PAPER AMERICANA.

rate of half a million a year—made up more than 70 percent of Chicago's population. In the Massachusetts textile mills thread was being spun by the mile by a work force that was 60 percent Irish. Many of the immigrants were Irish and Germans who had fled famine and depression in Europe. There were Jews, Italians, Poles, Lithuanians, and Greeks, too, crowding and squeezing into wooden shanties in soot-blackened ghettos along streets clogged with carriages and horse trolleys. From the burgs and shtetls of Europe, the peasantry perceived America as the land of the wealthy, and once they reached the Atlantic shore, they wasted little time rolling up their sleeves and hustling. Turn-of-the-century *Chicago Evening Post* columnist Finley Peter Dunne summarized the drive that made the New World go 'round in the droll wit of his classic creation, Mr. Dooley, the saloon keeper with the tart Irish brogue: "The crownin' wurruk iv our civilization is th' cash raygister."

As the railroads pushed west, the bankers stalked like bloodhounds. In 1854, Chicago boasted twenty-five investment bankers, compared to the eighteen in New York and ten in Boston. Investment bankers were—and still are today—the middlemen between companies that sell stock and the public that wants to buy. For a fee, they advise companies on matters of timing, pricing, and the issue size of a stock offering. Investment bankers proliferated in the mid-1850s because railroads were the growth industry of the nineteenth century and represented one-fourth of the total active capital in the country. Nearly half of all corporations chartered in America between 1800 and 1860 took place in

the decade of the fifties and most were railroads. Industry was being run by businessmen who kept one eye on the ledger and one on the stock exchange.

The publicly held corporation was as essential to railroad construction as the track was to railroad operation. Huge fortunes were required, far beyond the means of any single person or small group. In 1845, the only Americans worth more than one million dollars were John Jacob and William B. Astor, Peter G. Stuyvesant, and Cornelius Vanderbilt. On the other hand, in 1830, to build the Baltimore & Ohio—America's first steam railway—cost $15 million; the New York Central, $30 million; and the Erie, $25 million. Financing of these rail lines would have been impossible without appealing to the public purse.

By 1838 the Western Railroad in Massachusetts had 2,331 stockholders. The New York Central in 1853 had 2,445. The Pennsylvania Railroad, with more than 2,600 shareholders, was financed by the house-to-house sale of stock. The charters of these companies allowed shareholders to vote either at stockholders' meetings or by proxies. Such tools as non-voting stock, management shares, and stock options were not yet devised. But diffuse stockholders indeed marked a significant change in the corporate boardroom: Ownership was separated from control.

This seminal period for the spread of corporate stocks and bonds among a growing investment-minded public, spawned dare-anything manipulators like Jay Gould and Jim Fisk, a pair of Picassos in the art of boodle. During this time merchants, financiers, manufacturers, and developers

ABOVE: NATIVE AMERICANS FIGURED PROMINENTLY ON THE VIGNETTES OF MANY NINETEENTH-CENTURY STOCK CERTIFICATES—ESPECIALLY RAILROAD SHARES. ABOVE ARE FOUR VIEWS OF CORPORATE AMERICA DURING AN ERA OF BRUTAL EXPANSIONISM. UPPER LEFT: THE WHITE WOODSMAN VANQUISHING THE INDIANS; UPPER RIGHT: THE WHITE MAN COMMUNICATING PEACEFULLY; LOWER LEFT: HUNTERS OF THE PLAINS; LOWER RIGHT: SUBDUED AND CONTEMPLATIVE. TOWARD THE TURN OF THE CENTURY THE INDIAN WAS RENDERED AS A HEROIC FIGURE—FROM CHARLES SKINNER'S INDIAN HEAD ON THE 1893 WORLD'S COLUMBIAN EXPOSITION TICKET TO WILLIAM FORD'S INDIAN CHIEF ON THE ATCHINSON, TOPEKA AND SANTA FE RAILWAY STOCK CERTIFICATE.

The Pettengill Telegraph Revolver Company

CAPITAL STOCK 1,000,000 DOLLARS.

SHARES $100 EACH.

$5000   50 Shares.

New York, March 9th 1858

Be it known, That C. S. Pettengill is entitled to Fifty Shares of the Capital Stock of THE PETTENGILL TELEGRAPH REVOLVER COMPANY transferable only on the Books of the Company by himior by his legal representative upon surrender of this Certificate.

A.G. Whiton Secretary   David Austen Jr President.

For value received hereby sell assign and transfer to the Shares named in the above certificate. Witness hand and seal this day of 185 C. S. Pettengill

American Express Company

Capital Stock 7,500 Shares.

SHARES 100 DOLLARS EACH.

American Express Company.

Nº 108

4 SHARES.

This Certifies, That *John A Delanoi* is entitled to *Four* Shares of the Capital Stock of the American Express Company and transferable only on the Books of said Company on surrender of this Certificate.

And it is hereby further Certified That pursuant to the articles of association of said American Express Co. said Stock is subject to assessment for all losses or other liabilities incurred by said Company and that each and every assignee thereof from and after the date of the assignment becomes thereby a member of said Company, subject to all the liabilities and entitled to all the rights of an original member thereof.

In Witness Whereof, The said Company have caused this Certificate to be signed by their President and Secretary and countersigned by the Treasurer at the Office of the Company. New York, this ___ day of *March* 1854

Wm F Fargo Secretary

COUNTERSIGNED.

Alex Holland Treasurer

Henry Wells President.

Baker & Durekinck 158 Pearl St. N.Y.

began using checks canceled through central clearing-houses, rather than cumbersome commercial paper, and commodity transactions were increasingly being conducted through negotiable contracts rather than in raw products themselves. Now people were dealing in the liquid rights to property—paper money, mortgages, land warrants, futures contracts on commodities, stocks, and bonds—rather than in real property itself. Deals could be consummated by negotiable paper. Clearly the premium had shifted to money wealth away from landed wealth with railroad speculation leading the way.

Between 1850 and 1857, about twenty-three hundred miles of railroad tracks were built annually at a total cost of $60 million. The coasts of a half-wild continent were linked in 1869 when the tracks of the Central Pacific and Union Pacific Railroads were joined at Promontory Point, Utah, linking America and accelerating its commerce. From the West Coast alone, some fifty-three million pounds of commodities began pouring into Chicago yearly, including everything from borax to butter, and wood to wine. And from there the goods were shipped to all points east.

Chicago's stockyards bulged with eight hundred thousand head of cattle shipped out of Dodge and Abilene for New York, Philadelphia, Boston, and other points east. To get those cattle to market, cowboys relied on chuck wagons, the kind built by Studebaker Company (that would one day make cars, too) that sold for seventy-five dollars each.

The month-long trip from San Francisco to St. Louis, Chicago, and other Midwest terminals by the combination of railroad and rickety stagecoach was now cut by a week by train, which shuttled big-city ideas to small towns via hungry salesmen with order blanks for every product imaginable. By 1876 there were forty-six million Americans and fifty thousand miles of railroad track—more than in any other nation—linking ports, factory towns, and farming centers with textiles from New England, steel from Pittsburgh, longhorn beef from Texas, shoes from St. Louis, wheat from

ABOVE: A VIGNETTE OF THE NATION'S FIRST STEEL BRIDGE. THE 1500-FOOT EADS BRIDGE, WHICH OPENED IN 1874, SPANNED THE MISSISSIPPI RIVER FROM ST. LOUIS TO ILLINOIS AND TOOK SEVEN YEARS TO BUILD. FROM A MISSISSIPPI AND MISSOURI RAILROAD SHARE. COURTESY GEORGE LABARRE.

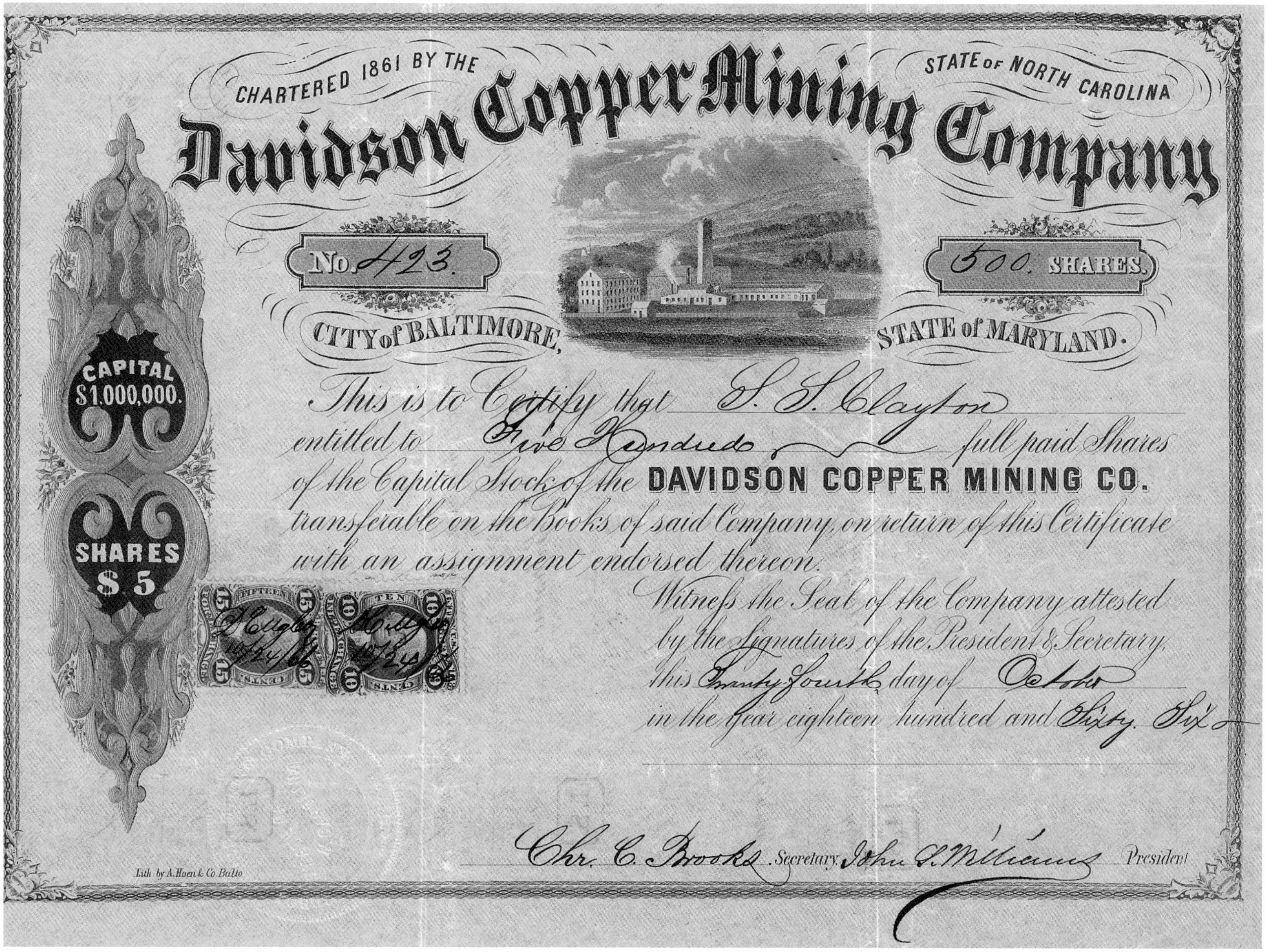

CHARTERED 1861 BY THE
STATE OF NORTH CAROLINA

Davidson Copper Mining Company

No. 493.

500 SHARES.

CITY OF BALTIMORE,

STATE OF MARYLAND.

CAPITAL $1,000,000.

SHARES $5

This is to Certify that S. S. Clayton entitled to Five Hundred full paid Shares of the Capital Stock of the DAVIDSON COPPER MINING CO. transferable on the Books of said Company, on return of this Certificate with an assignment endorsed thereon.

Witness the Seal of the Company attested by the Signatures of the President & Secretary, this Twenty Fourth day of October in the year eighteen hundred and Sixty Six

Chr. C. Brooks, Secretary   John S. Williams, President

Lith. by A. Hoen & Co. Balto.

Philadelphia and Southern Mail Steamship Company

EACH SHARE $250.

Authorized Capital, $1,500,000.

No.

Shares

This Certifies that Samuel J. Sharpless is entitled to Ten Shares in the Capital Stock of the Philadelphia & Southern Mail Steamship Co. Transferable only on the Books of the Company in Person or by Attorney on return of this Certificate. Witness the seal of said Company and the signatures of the President and Treasurer at Philadelphia, June 8 1876

Charles S Teal Treasurer

S. Flanagan President.

J. Raebuler, Goldsmiths Hall opposite Post Office, Phil.

PHILADELPHIA SOUTHERN MAIL STEAMSHIP COMPANY

ABOVE: THE U.S. GOVERNMENT AUTHORIZED THE FIRST OCEAN-MAIL CONTRACTS IN 1845, LONG BEFORE THE BUILDING OF THE RAILROADS AND THE PANAMA CANAL. TWO YEARS LATER THE FIRST TRANSATLANTIC STEAMERS WERE INTRODUCED. WITH THE ADVENT OF STEAMS ENGINES, COMPANIES BEGAN CARRYING MAIL ACROSS THE ATLANTIC AND TO SAN FRANCISCO, AN ARDUOUS JOURNEY THAT REQUIRED NAVIGATING CAPE HORN AT THE TIP OF SOUTH AMERICA. THE VIGNETTE ON THIS 1876 SHARE ILLUSTRATES A TYPICAL SHIP OF THE ERA, MODELED ON THE SAILING SHIP IT REPLACED, BUT STILL CARRYING AUXILIARY SAILS ON ITS MAST. COURTESY OF DAVID M. BEACH.

Certify that *William Scha*

One Hundred

OF THE

TAL

STA

nt **Mining Compa**

transferable only on the Books

Company, in person or by Attorney, on surr

INCORPORATED UNDER THE LAWS OF UTAH.

This is to Certify that *William Scharp* is entitled to *One Hundred* Shares

NUMBER 3090 OF THE CAPITAL

STOCK OF THE — 100 —

SHARES $1 EACH

CAPITAL $500,000.

Stormont Mining Company of Utah

transferable only on the Books of the Company, in person, or by Attorney, on surrender of this Certificate.

In Witness whereof the President and Secretary have hereunto affixed their signatures at its Office in the City of Salt Lake, this 9th day of Dec. 1886.

C. J. Casserly, Secretary pt.

Chas. S. Hinchman, President

American Bank Note Co. New-York.

HARRISBURG DISTRICT. WASHINGTON Co., UTAH.

STORMONT MINING COMPANY OF UTAH

ABOVE AND OPPOSITE: STORMONT MINING COMPANY OF UTAH (1886) IS FAMOUS FOR THIS SINGULAR VIGNETTE— TWO INFANTS PLAYING ON TWO SILVER DOLLARS. FOUR CORNER VIGNETTES COMPLETE THE PAGE ACCENTED BY A COMPLEX BORDER WITH BOTH GEOMETRIC LATHING AND ENGRAVING. OUTSTANDING ROSETTE-LIKE CORNER PIECES HAVE LEAVES PROTRUDING INTO THE CENTER PORTION OF THE SHARE. COURTESY OF STOCK SEARCH INTERNATIONAL, INC.

Iowa, and cotton from Louisiana. America celebrated the centennial of the signing of the Declaration of Independence and one-time ferry boat captain Cornelius Vanderbilt, who had amassed the world's largest fortune—an astounding $103 million—celebrated his eighty-second birthday. But the depression of 1873 still lingered. And so did the scars of the Civil War, with Florida, Louisiana, and South Carolina still under martial law. The sea of buffalo—some 75 million of them slaughtered for their hides—no longer roamed the Great Plains and most Native Americans had been pushed into pockets of despair, their tribes scattered like chaff in the wind.

The West was still wild, an expanse of desolate plains and harsh mountains referred to in some geography books of the day as the "Great American Desert." Before the rail union between east and west, there were few cities between Chicago and San Francisco at all, and none whose population numbered more than five thousand people. Suddenly, towns sprouted over the vast prairie where only gophers and jack rabbits had lived. Railroad euphoria spread across the nation, bolstered by President James A. Garfield, who her-

alded the train as "the greatest centralizing force of modern times."

As railroads prodded Americans on a faster and farther track, technology created a bumper crop of gizmos and gadgets that were introduced to expand man's output. In the 1840s some 5,942 new patents were issued. In the 1850s the number quadrupled to include wheat thrashers, mechanical drills, water wheels, steam engines, and pumps. Cyrus McCormack's Chicago factory sold 1,558 reapers and sowers in 1854 and was planning for 3,000 machines in 1855. Before the Civil War, it took sixty-one hours of labor to produce one acre of hand-grown wheat. By the late 1800s, machinery yielded the same amount of wheat in under three-and-a-half hours. In 1890, a machine patented by James Bonsack could make more than twelve thousand cigarettes an hour, a forty-fold increase over the hand-labored

ABOVE, LEFT TO RIGHT: ULYSSES S. GRANT (1822–1885), U.S. GENERAL AND EIGHTEENTH PRESIDENT; CORNELIUS VANDERBILT (1794–1877), FINANCIER BORN IN STATEN ISLAND, NEW YORK; AND JAMES GARFIELD (1831–1881), U.S. STATESMAN AND TWENTIETH PRESIDENT. COURTESY OF AMERICAN BANK NOTE COMPANY.

STATES OF IOWA AND MISSOURI

Nº 686 Nº 686

Chicago & South Western

American Bank Note Co. New York

Shares

Shares

RAILWAY COMPANY

CHARTER PERPETUAL

Register

This Certifies that

entitled to

Shares of One Hundred Dollars each in the Capital Stock of the Chicago and Southwestern Railway Company, a Corporation created by and existing under the Laws of the States of Iowa and Missouri, transferable in person or by attorney on the Books of the Company at its Office in the City of New York, on a surrender of this Certificate. In Witness Whereof

Countersigned & Registered

The said Company have caused this Certificate to be signed by its President & Treasurer. Dated at the Transfer Office in the City of New York, this _____ day of _____ 18__

TREAS^R

PRESIDENT.

REVENUE STAMP PRESENTED FOR REDEMPTION

CHICAGO & SOUTH WESTERN RAILWAY COMPANY

ABOVE: THIS CHICAGO & SOUTH WESTERN RAILWAY SHARE IS IN MINT CONDITION BECAUSE IT WAS NEVER ISSUED. A HOARD OF UNISSUED SHARES MAY EXIST AFTER A COMPANY GOES BANKRUPT, OUT OF BUSINESS, OR IS TAKEN OVER BY ANOTHER FIRM. ALTHOUGH NEVER USED, SUCH SHARES ARE SOMETIMES SIGNED BY OFFICERS IN ANTICIPATION OF THEIR ISSUANCE. THE CHARM OF THIS CERTIFICATE IS IN ITS VARIETY OF COLOR AND VIGNETTES: THE LOCOMOTIVE, THE ALLEGORICAL CHERUBS, AND THE SEALS REPRESENTING THE STATES OF IOWA AND MISSOURI. COURTESY OF JOHN A. PARKER.

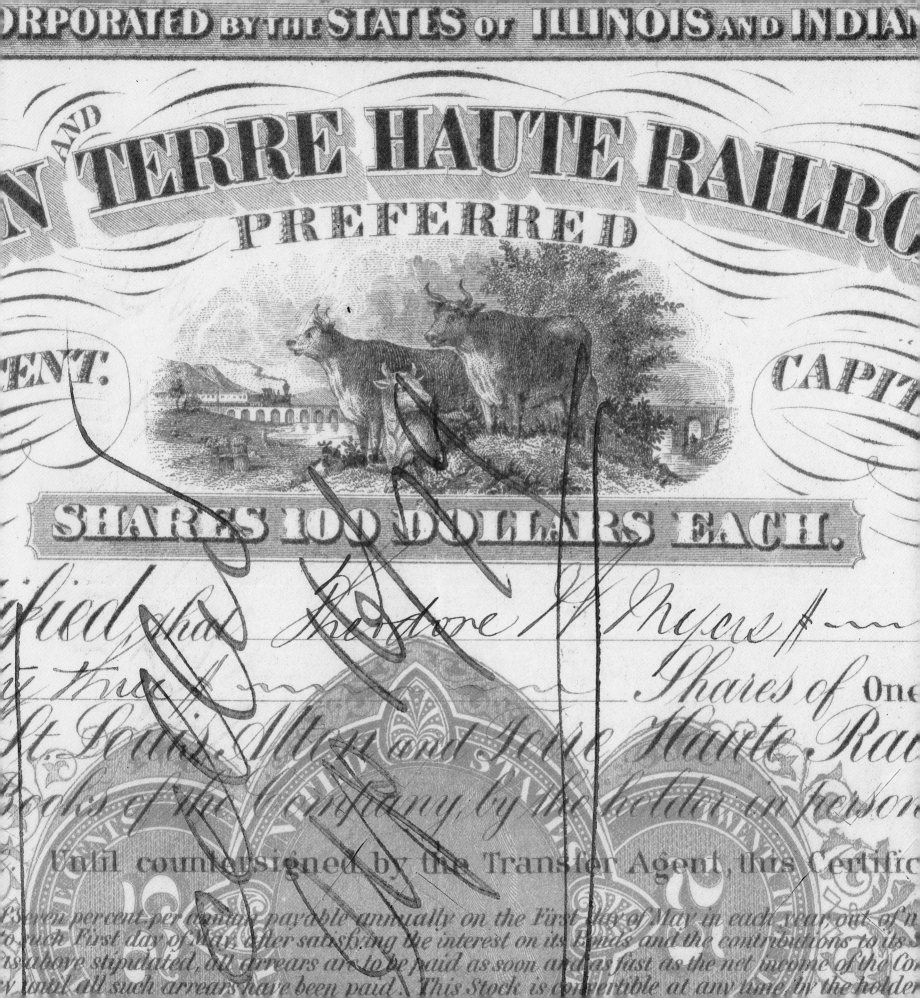

MERGENTHALER LINOTYPE COMPANY

ABOVE: FOR MORE THAN FOUR HUNDRED YEARS AFTER THE INVENTION OF PRINTING, ALL TYPE WAS SET BY HAND. IN THE NINETEENTH CENTURY, TYPESETTING MACHINES WERE INVENTED, THOUGH NONE WERE SUFFICIENT FOR COMMERCIAL OPERATION UNTIL THE LINOTYPE WAS INVENTED IN 1886. THE LINOTYPE CAST A SOLID BAR, OR SLUG, OF RAISED LETTERS IN A LINE—A LINE OF TYPE MOLDED FROM MELTED LEAD. THIS SHARE IS FROM 1896. COURTESY OF GEORGE LABARRE.

The New York and New Jersey Bridge Company of New York.

No. 175

THIS IS TO CERTIFY GENERAL MORTGAGE BONDS

ONE Coupon Bond of ONE THOUSAND DOLLARS

1000

NEW YORK AND NEW JERSEY BRIDGE COMPANY

ABOVE: A DECADE AFTER THE BROOKLYN BRIDGE WAS BUILT, SPANS OF STEEL LINKED NEW YORK WITH NEW JERSEY. THIS NEW YORK AND NEW JERSEY BRIDGE COMPANY OF NEW YORK BOND CERTIFICATE WAS ISSUED IN 1892.

DESIGNED AND PRINTED BY THE NEW YORK BANK NOTE COMPANY, WHICH CEASED OPERATIONS SIX YEARS LATER, THE CERTIFICATE'S VIGNETTE DEPICTS A PASTORAL VIEW OF NEW YORK HARBOR, WELL BEFORE THE LANDSCAPE WAS

CHANGED BY SKYSCRAPERS. THE CERTIFICATE ALSO FEATURES A TEXTURED, ENGRAVED BACKGROUND THAT, WHEN VIEWED UNDER GLASS, REVEALS HAND LETTERING. COURTESY OF GEORGE HEWITSON COLLECTIBLES.

Elsewhere engineers and architects began to use steel to support buildings so tall they were called skyscrapers. Back east a decade later,

LEFT: PORTRAIT OF THOMAS EDISON (1847–1931), INVENTOR AND PHYSICIST. COURTESY OF AMERICAN BANK NOTE COMPANY.

a clever and enterprising business journalist who covered Wall Street with his *Customer's Afternoon Letter* had an idea to devise a market average of stocks that represented widely traded issues of financially sound companies. His name was Charles Dow and he published the first Dow average on July 3, 1884 (on that day the average was 69.93). The average was made up of just two industrial stocks (Pacific Mail Steamship and Western Union) and nine railroad stocks (Chicago & Northwestern, Delaware, Lackawanna & Western, Lake Shore, Louisville & Nashville, Missouri Pacific, New York Central, Northern Pacific preferred, St. Paul, and Union Pacific). The list clearly indicated the continued dominance of the railroad industry on America's financial landscape. Dow's *Customer's Afternoon Letter*, of course, was the forerunner of the *Wall Street Journal*.

output a decade earlier. In 1870, there was no such thing as a telephone, but by 1900 there were nineteen thousand telephone operators and two hundred American cities with thirty thousand electric trolley cars. The population rose from 39 million to 76 million, along with the increase in per capita income from $779 to $1,164.

Meanwhile a fiery steel process burst out of the gaslight age when Ulysses S. Grant was brooding in the White House. An Englishman named Henry Bessemer devised a method by which a blast of air was blown through molten pig iron to cheapen the process of steel making and to hasten the coming of the Machine Age. On July 4, 1874 the new fifteen hundred–foot Eads Bridge spanning the Mississippi River from St. Louis to Illinois was opened. From then on, steel was the heart and spine of city building.

As large sections of the big cities were becoming ethnically rich but pocket-poor, more and more farmers were becoming urban dwellers, pushed off the land by mechanized farm implements, built by the Harvesters and Deeres, that enabled one man to do the work of six. Despite the farm exodus, in 1890 the nation's eight million farm workers still outnumbered jobholders in all other industries. Few farmers were turning profits, however, resulting in a Populist revolt that focused on enforcing the Interstate Commerce Act of 1887, which placed

Edison Phonograph Works

No. 68

30 — Shares

EDISON PHONOGRAPH WORKS

Incorporated under the Laws of the State of New Jersey.

This is to Certify that _Mrs Thos A. Edison_ is entitled to _Thirty_ Shares in the Capital Stock of the EDISON PHONOGRAPH WORKS transferable only on the Books of the Company, in person, or by Attorney on the surrender of this Certificate.

NEW JERSEY, _Nov 10th_ 1888

CAPITAL STOCK $300,000.

SHARES $100 EACH.

John B. Powers & Son, Stationers, 101 Chambers St., N.Y.

Treasurer.

Thos A Edison

President.

EDISON PHONOGRAPH WORKS

ABOVE: IN 1869 AT AGE TWENTY-TWO THOMAS EDISON SOLD HIS FIRST PATENT, THE STOCK TICKER, WHICH WAS IMMEDIATELY USED ON WALL STREET. THE LIGHT BULB, PHONOGRAPH, STORAGE BATTERY, AND FILM PROJECTOR FOLLOWED, ALONG WITH MORE THAN ONE THOUSAND OTHER PATENTS HE HELD AT THE TIME OF HIS DEATH IN 1931. HE FOUNDED THE EDISON PHONOGRAPH WORKS IN THE 1880S FOR DEVELOPMENT AND PRODUCTION OF THE PHONOGRAPH. BY 1910 THE PHONOGRAPH WORKS BECAME A CRITICAL PART OF THE EDISON EMPIRE, BRINGING IN MORE THAN $1 MILLION A YEAR, ENABLING HIM TO FINANCE HIS OTHER VENTURES. COURTESY OF GEORGE LABARRE.

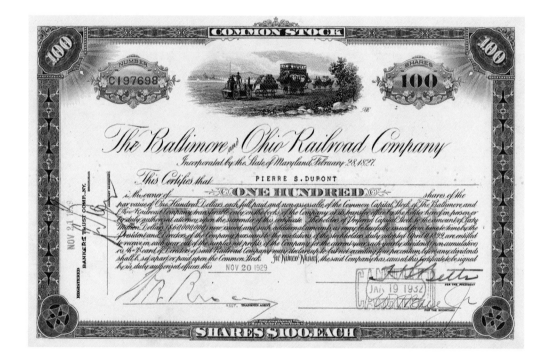

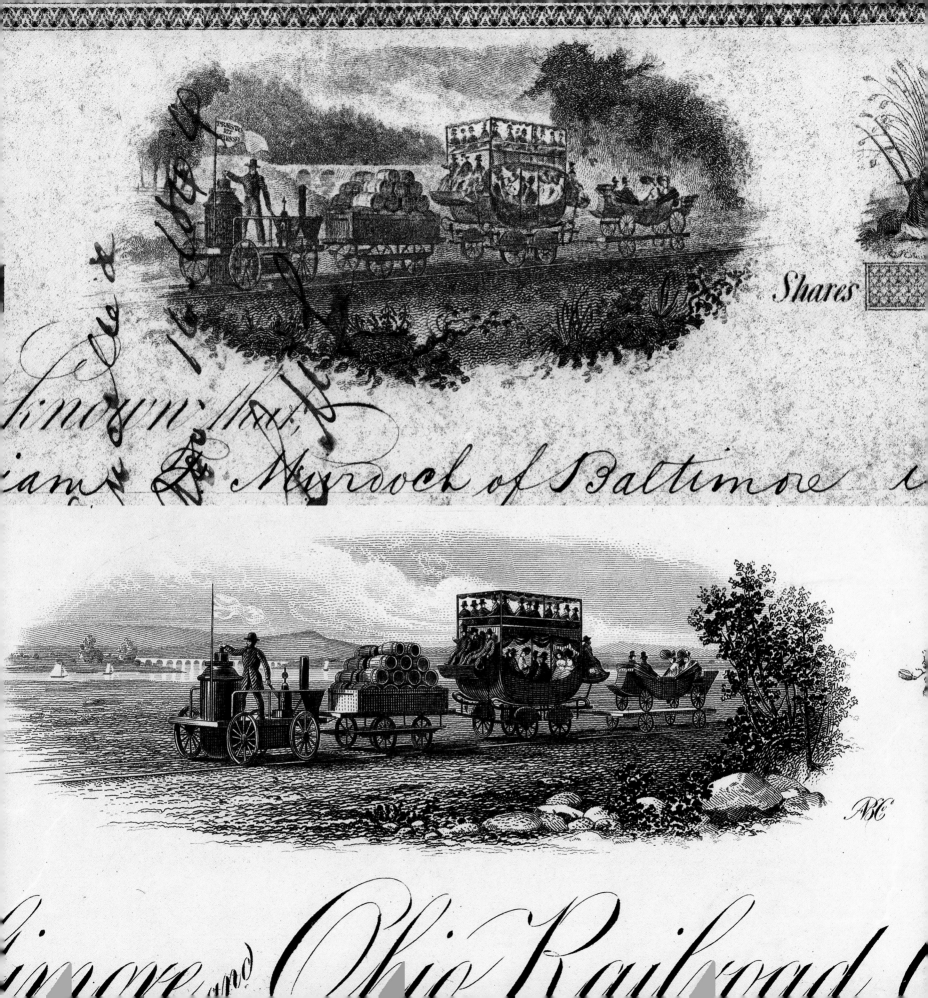

Shares

...known Mr...
...iam H. Murdoch of Baltimore...

Baltimore and Ohio Railroad

controls over railroads, and the Sherman Antitrust Act of 1890, which tried to harness monopolies. At first clever lawyers found plenty of loopholes in the act. But as time went on the muckraking press added monopolies to the lengthy list of public evils, and the politicians tightened the laws.

The exchanges, on the other hand, had support in high places. The very man who coined the word "muckraker" in his pledge to bust the trusts, spoke out in favor of the exchanges. "The great bulk of the business transacted on the exchanges is not only legitimate," President Theodore Roosevelt said, "but is necessary to the working of our modern industrial system, and extreme care would have to be taken not to interfere with this business in doing away with the bucket-shop type of operations."

Bucket shops were the bookies of their day. Only instead of betting on horses, it was stocks or commodities. Wagers could be made on current prices of stocks without any intention of buying them. If a person bet the price would go up, the bucket-shop operator would take the opposite position and vice versa. The loser would pay the difference as reflected in the New York Stock Exchange price quotations. Bucket shops were nothing more than gambling dens that hurt the integrity of the exchanges. (The term "bucket shop" first appeared in the United States in the 1870s, but was coined in London fifty years earlier and grew out of the habits of swillers rather than speculators. Beer beggars would roam the streets with buckets in hand, draining every keg they'd come across. They would then park themselves in small darkened dens and pass the bucket like a loving cup as each took a pull. The dens came to be called bucket shops and eventually were used as a byword of reproach to small places where grain and stock deals were counterfeited. Bucket shops in one form or another lingered into the 1920s before authorities closed them down for good.)

While businessmen banded together to form trade associations to bolster fair trade practices, labor disorders—the Haymarket Riot and Pullman Strike among them—ricocheted across American cities in the late 1800s, shaking the foundation of business. By this time, American sectionalism had been replaced by a new spirit of nationalism, created by a blend of transportation and communication: completion of the transcontinental railroad, the telegraph and telephone system, news services like the Associated Press, and national markets for magazines and books. The boundaries shrank even further as manufacturers churned out standard factory products. And around this time Thomas Edison made his contribution to the securities industry with his invention of the stock ticker, which spun out stock prices on continuous rolls of paper one tick at a time.

The railroad industry, too, fine-tuned itself with new innovations. Eli Janning created the automatic coupler that held rail cars together like a handsake; George Westinghouse perfected a breaking system using air pressure; Granville Woods devised a way to send electrical impulses through track, enabling trains to communicate with each other; and Elijah McCoy patented an engine lubricating system so dependable that it came to be known as "the real McCoy."

UNITED STATES GUANO COMPANY

ABOVE: THROUGHOUT THE NINETEENTH CENTURY THERE WERE MANY COMPANIES THAT MINED AND MARKETED THE EXCREMENT OF BIRDS AND BATS AS FERTILIZER CALLED GUANO (A SPANISH WORD FROM THE PERUVIAN *HUANU*, MEANING DUNG). THE UNITED STATES GUANO COMPANY WOULD MINE THE DROPPINGS, RICH IN NITRATES, PHOSPHATES, AND OXALATES, ON ISLANDS OFF THE COST OF PERU AND AFRICA. THIS CERTIFICATE'S VIGNETTES (1859) DEPICT WHAT THE COMPANY DOES. THE BALD EAGLE EVOKES "AMERICAN"; THE ENGRAVED PORTRAITS ARE OF ITS FOUNDERS; THE BIG SHIPS TRANSPORT THE GUANO; AND THE FARMER USES IT FOR HIS FIELDS. COURTESY OF GEORGE LABARRE.

SHARES $100 EACH   **SHARES $100 EACH**

Nº 467   50 *Shares*

CHICAGO AND CANADA SOUTHERN
Railway   **Company.**

This Certifies that N. Wilbur Smith is Entitled to Fifty Shares of One hundred dollars each in the Capital Stock of the Chicago and Canada Southern Railway Company, transferable in person or by Attorney on the Books of the Company at its office in the City of New York, or at any Transfer Agency established by the Company, only on the surrender of this Certificate.

In Witness Whereof, the said Company has caused this Certificate to be signed by its President and Treasurer. Dated at the Transfer Office in the City of New York, this Thirteenth day of March 1879.

_____ Treasurer.   _____ President.

CHICAGO AND CANADA SOUTHERN RAILWAY COMPANY

ABOVE: INCORPORATED IN 1871 TO BUILD A 250-MILE RAIL LINE FROM DETROIT, MICHIGAN, TO CHICAGO, ILLINOIS, THE CHICAGO AND CANADA SOUTHERN RAILWAY NEVER GOT ROLLING. TWO YEARS LATER, IT HAD MANAGED TO LAY DOWN JUST 67 MILES OF TRACK AND WAS ACQUIRED BY THE LAKE SHORE AND MICHIGAN RAILWAY COMPANY, WHOSE CHAIRMAN WAS WILLIAM KISSAM VANDERBILT, THE GRANDSON OF CORNELIUS VANDERBILT. BY 1886 THE CHICAGO AND CANADA HAD YET TO MAKE A PROFIT AND HAD BEEN IN DEFAULT ON ITS BONDS. IT FILED FOR BANKRUPTCY AND CLOSED DOWN. COURTESY OF GEORGE LABARRE.

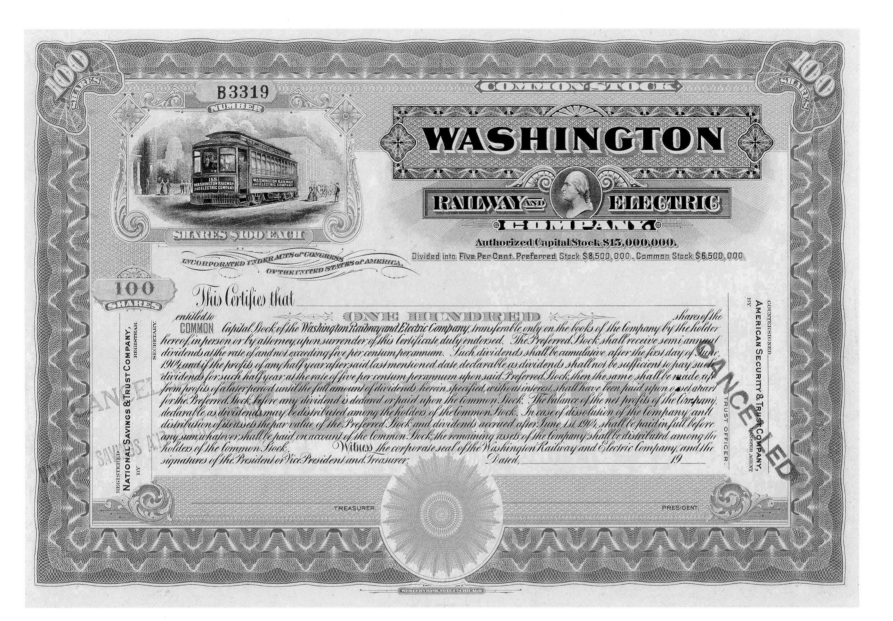

WASHINGTON RAILWAY AND ELECTRIC COMPANY

SHARES $5.00 EACH

ONI WIRELESS TELEGRAPH CO

OF AMERICA

that   BILLETT, CAMPBELL & GRENFELL

----------FIVE----------

Five Dollars ($5.00) each, fully paid, and non-assessable in the C
Wireless Telegraph Company of America, transferable on th
in person, or by duly authorized attorney, on surrender of th
endorsed. This Certificate shall not be valid until
Agent and the Registrar

SHARES $5.00 EACH

CERTIFICATE FOR LESS THAN 100 SHARES

CERTIFICATE FOR LESS THAN 100 SHARES

NUMBER 023730

SHARES

MARCONI WIRELESS TELEGRAPH COMPANY
OF AMERICA

INCORPORATED UNDER THE LAWS .... OF THE STATE OF ....

This is to Certify that **BILLETT, CAMPBELL & GRENFELL**

is the owner of -------------------FIVE------------- shares of the par

value of Five Dollars ($5.00) each, fully paid, and non-assessable in the Capital Stock of
Marconi Wireless Telegraph Company of America, transferable on the books of the
Company in person, or by duly authorized attorney, on surrender of this Certificate
properly endorsed. This Certificate shall not be valid until countersigned by the
Transfer Agent and the Registrar.

Witness the seal of the Company and the signatures of its duly authorized officers
this .... day of FEB 17 1913

TREASURER.   VICE-PRESIDENT.

AMERICAN BANK NOTE COMPANY, NEW YORK.

CAPITAL STOCK

CANCELLED

MARCONI WIRELESS TELEGRAPH COMPANY OF AMERICA

OPPOSITE AND ABOVE: THE MARCONI WIRELESS TELEGRAPH COMPANY WAS INCORPORATED IN NOVEMBER 1899 TO OPERATE THE WIRELESS TELEGRAPH IN THE UNITED STATES UNDER THE PATENTS OF GUGLIELMO MARCONI, THE ITALIAN INVENTOR, AND THOMAS EDISON. MARCONI SERVED AS THE COMPANY'S PRESIDENT. BY 1912 MARCONI WIRELESS HAD ACQUIRED MOST OF ITS COMPETITORS, HAD SIXTY LAND STATIONS ACROSS THE U.S., AND HAD EQUIPPED OVER FIVE HUNDRED MERCHANT STEAMSHIPS, INCLUDING THE *TITANIC*. COURTESY OF GEORGE LaBARRE.

ACK TRUCK

INCORPORATED UNDER THE LAWS OF NEW YORK.

CHAPTER FOUR

Small businessmen, through their trade groups, had a single-minded purpose: to survive in an era when monopoly was the mother of expansion. Practically every entrepreneur faced the recurrent pattern of the nineteenth century: first the machine, then the monopoly. Even the mundane seasonal egg business was drastically altered with the advent of mechanical refrigeration. Steel, oil, railroads, utilities, and meat packing were among the industries dominated by impatient, tyrannical individuals who pushed themselves and their competitors to the limits of endurance with new machines and new ways of raising capital. They squeezed small competitors into submission in an age of enterprise when it was difficult and even impossible to carve a commercial niche among the Cornelius Vanderbilts, Philip Armours, Gustavus Swifts, Marshall Fields, Cyrus McCormicks, William Wrigleys, George Pullmans, Andrew Carnegies, and J. Pierpont Morgans.

BROKEN TRUST

Such economic titans were confident, egotistical, single-minded, and full of play with money and minds. They knew how to romance capitalism and pluck the strings of greed among potential investors. Pragmatically and unemotionally they were energized by the panic and financial chaos of others as they moved from one venture to another like sharks in constant motion in search of their next corporate meal. They were Parker Brothers originals who made monopoly a real game through financial pools, interlocking directorates, and trusts. Consolidation was the name of the game. In the late 1880s, 40 percent of worldwide demand for petroleum was met by the output of three refineries instead of fifty a few years before.

By the middle of the nineteenth century it seemed America—the great melting pot of humanity—had traded in its hold on meritocracy for royalty given the dominance of a new type of gentry. Railroad barons, land barons, cattle barons, newspaper barons, and robber barons were the movers and shakers in the peerage of industrial America. The rest was the working class. But even the working class had a chance to invest in the nation's economic future by buying stocks and bonds if they could afford them. What an *if*. For instance, department store tycoon Marshall Field, whose company was still private, was making five hundred dollars an hour in 1880, while most

OPPOSITE: EVER SINCE ITS TRUCKS FIRST HIT THE ROAD IN 1900, THE PHRASE "BUILT LIKE A MACK TRUCK" HAS BEEN USED TO DESCRIBE ANYTHING BIG, HEAVY DUTY, AND DEPENDABLE. COURTESY GEORGE LABARRE.

NUMBER
NF 3162

SHARES
1

Ringling Bros.— Barnum & Bailey Combined Shows, Inc.

INCORPORATED UNDER THE LAWS OF THE STATE OF DELAWARE

COMMON STOCK

THIS CERTIFICATE IS TRANSFERABLE
IN THE CITIES
OF NEW YORK,
HOUSTON OR
SAN FRANCISCO

SEE REVERSE FOR
CERTAIN
DEFINITIONS

THIS CERTIFIES THAT   is the record holder of

ONE

FULL-PAID AND NON-ASSESSABLE SHARES, PAR VALUE 50¢ PER SHARE, OF THE COMMON STOCK OF
RINGLING BROS.-BARNUM & BAILEY COMBINED SHOWS, INC., transferable on the share register of the corporation in person or by duly
authorized attorney upon surrender of this certificate properly endorsed.
This certificate is not valid unless countersigned by the Transfer Agent and registered by the Registrar.
Witness the facsimile signatures of its duly authorized officers.

Dated: MAY 1 2 1970

Lewis Jacobs
Secretary

President

Registered:
CHEMICAL BANK
(New York)
Registrar
Authorized Signature
By

Countersigned:
CHEMICAL BANK
(New York) Transfer Agent
Authorized Signature
By

THE GREATEST SHOW ON EARTH®

AMERICAN BANK NOTE COMPANY.

© 1966, 1969 RINGLING BROS.—BARNUM & BAILEY COMBINED SHOWS, INC.

RINGLING BROS.–BARNUM & BAILEY COMBINED SHOWS, INC.

ABOVE: THIS STOCK CERTIFICATE (1970) IS AS COLORFUL AS THE SHOW AND THE COMPANY'S HISTORY. BEGUN IN 1882 BY THE FIVE RINGLING BROTHERS, THE RINGLING BROTHERS CARNIVAL OF FUN TURNED INTO THE RINGLING CIRCUS IN 1884. THE BIG TOP AND MENAGERIE WERE CARRIED FROM TOWN TO TOWN IN A PROCESSION OF WAGONS. BY 1890, WHEN IT BEGAN TO BE KNOWN AS "THE GREATEST SHOW ON EARTH," THE CIRCUS HAD TO MOVE BY RAIL. IN 1907 RINGLING ACQUIRED COMPETITOR BARNUM AND BAILEY AND CONTINUED TO BE INDEPENDENT UNTIL 1971, WHEN MATTEL INC. ACQUIRED THE CIRCUS THROUGH AN EXCHANGE OF STOCK. COURTESY GEORGE LABARRE.

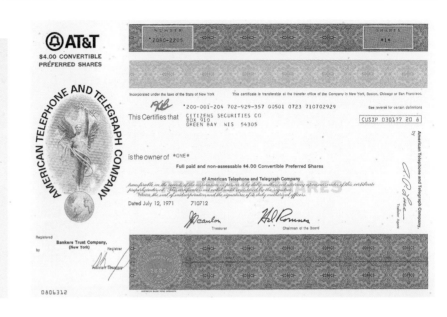

of his employees were making about twelve dollars for a fifty-nine-hour week.

The East was still fascinated by the West and its legends became a prime market for pulp fiction. In the 1870s and 1880s, the publisher Beadle and Adams churned out more than two thousand dime novels whose heroes were both bad guys and good guys like Jesse James, Wild Bill Hickok, Billy the Kid, Denver Dan, Fancy Frank, Kit Carson, and Buffalo Bill. (One prolific author, Colonel Prentiss Ingraham, wrote one hundred and twenty dime novels about Buffalo Bill alone.) To give the fantasies a bit of virtual reality with sound, sight, and smell, along came William F. (Buffalo Bill) Cody, the greatest merchandiser of the live Western show that featured sharpshooter Annie Oakley, mock attacks by real Indian braves, and some fancy riding and roping by Buffalo Bill himself. In 1883, he sold stock to the public in Buffalo Bill's Wild West Company to finance his touring extravaganza across the United States and Europe as well. The cash flow also permitted Buffalo Bill to acquire the rival show of Pawnee Bill, another myth-making promoter of the

West, just as in 1881 James Anthony Bailey had combined his circus with P. T. Barnum's to form "The Greatest Show On Earth." (In 1907, the Ringling Brothers, who formed their first circus in 1884, would take over Barnum & Bailey to form Ringling Bros. and Barnum & Bailey, also a publicly held company.)

Meanwhile economic cycles played no favorites. Two-thirds of the years between 1873 and 1894 were wracked by panic. The large manufacturers, just learning to operate at new levels of scale with high fixed costs, were particularly vulnerable. For example, in the language of the period and depending on the year, the steel industry was either "strained to utmost capacity" or "panic-stricken." The railroads, too, were walloped. In 1893—the year steel enabled Brooklyn to unite with Manhattan via its own bridge—after two decades

ABOVE: FOUR YEARS AFTER THE CONNECTICUT TELEPHONE SHARE WAS ISSUED, AT&T INCORPORATED IN 1885 AND EVENTUALLY BECAME THE WORLD'S LARGEST COMPANY. AT&T'S CORPORATE SYMBOL WAS ENGRAVED BY WILLIAM ADOLPH OF AMERICAN BANK NOTE. COURTESY OF DAVID M. BEACH (LEFT) AND GEORGE LABARRE (RIGHT).

DER THE LAWS

OF THE S

AN UNION TELEPHONE C

6% Non-Cumulative Preferred Stock $10,000,000.
Common Stock $15,000,000.

5,000,000.

CERTIFIES THAT *Jacob B Hillegas Esta*

he owner of Three Shares

MON *Capital Stock of the American Union Telephone Company,*

He transferable only on the books of the Corporation by the holder hereof in perso

rrender of this certificate, properly endorsed. The Preferred Stock shall

receive, out of the net earnings of the Company, a yearly non-cumulative div

re any dividend shall be set apart or paid on the Common Stock.

Witness Whereof, the said Corporation has caused this certificate to be signed by its

be sealed with the seal of the Company this

JUN 2 3 1900

NUMBER
B339

SHARES
3

INCORPORATED UNDER THE LAWS OF THE STATE OF PENNSYLVANIA

American Union Telephone Company

CAPITAL STOCK $25,000,000.

6% Non-Cumulative Preferred Stock $10,000,000.
Common Stock $15,000,000.

SHARES $100 EACH.

THIS CERTIFIES THAT *Jacob B Hillegas Estate*

is the owner of *Three* Shares of the COMMON Capital Stock of the American Union Telephone Company, fully paid and non-assessable, transferable only on the books of the Corporation by the holder hereof in person or by attorney, upon the surrender of this certificate properly endorsed. The Preferred Stock shall entitle the holder thereof to receive out of the net earnings of the Company a yearly non-cumulative dividend of six per centum, before any dividend shall be set apart or paid on the Common Stock.

In Witness Whereof, the said Corporation has caused this certificate to be signed by its duly authorized officers, and to be sealed with the seal of the Company, this JUN 23 1909

TREASURER

PRESIDENT

C135

CERTIFICATE FOR LESS THAN 100 SHARES

CERTIFICATE FOR LESS THAN 100 SHARES

NUMBER
00000

SHARES

INCORPORATED UNDER THE LAWS OF THE STATE OF ILLINOIS

SWIFT AND COMPANY

THIS CERTIFICATE IS TRANSFERABLE IN CHICAGO OR IN BOSTON

This Certifies that _____

is the owner of _____ full-paid and non-assessable shares of the par value of $25 each of the Capital Stock of Swift and Company transferable in person or by duly authorized attorney upon surrender of this Certificate properly endorsed. This Certificate is not valid unless countersigned by the Transfer Agent and registered by the Registrar. In Witness Whereof the Company has caused this Certificate to be executed by its duly authorized officers. Dated _____

CAPITAL STOCK

REGISTERED: THE NEW ENGLAND TRUST COMPANY (BOSTON) REGISTRAR

By

ASSISTANT SECRETARY

COUNTERSIGNED OLD COLONY TRUST COMPANY (BOSTON) TRANSFER AGENT

By

ASSISTANT SECRETARY

SPECIMEN

ASSISTANT SECRETARY

SPECIMEN

VICE PRESIDENT

AMERICAN BANK NOTE COMPANY.

of financial machinations and consolidations there were a dozen giant corporations with aggregate capital of less than a billion dollars. The railroads were the largest single type of enterprise in America next to farming. The major railroad lines—that employed tens of thousands of people—were overextended and overbuilt to the point that Midwestern shippers could choose among at least a half dozen carriers to the east coast. Since the railroads could not afford to let equipment sit idle, they drastically cut shipping rates. The result: Profits plunged followed by a wave of bankruptcies. And by 1895, some 169 railroads, representing nearly 20 percent of the nation's total rail mileage, were being operated by court-designated managers.

By 1904, more than a thousand separate railroad lines had consolidated into six huge concerns, each allied with the Morgan or Rockefeller interests. There were three hundred and eighteen industrial concerns at this time, including Morgan's United States Steel Corporation, which was capitalized at more than $1.4 billion, making it America's first billion-dollar company. Practically all the business was done through paper-shuffling, and stock was the grease to make merger wheels spin. It was used to buy up companies as well as to pay the promoters of the deals and the bankers who worked out the financial angles. Between 1898 and 1904 more than $4 billion in new securities were issued for industrial mergers alone. Such activity would eventually unleash the antitrust laws and the trust-busting fury of Theodore Roosevelt.

At the close of the nineteenth century there were no new prairies to cross with railroads, no inland markets to turn into factories, and no native tribes to vanquish. It seemed that the only new worlds to conquer were those beyond American shores, if for no other reason than to break the monotony of dollar chasing. In 1898, Teddy Roosevelt wanted a war to give the United States "something to think about which isn't material gain." He got his war in February of 1898 when the *Maine*, an American battleship, was sunk by an explosion while it lay in anchor in Havana harbor. With help from the newspaper barons of banality, yellow headlines whipped the public into a frenzy over the loss of 260 lives. And with the cry of "Remember the *Maine*," America was at war with Spain.

ABOVE: THE ALLEGORICAL VIGNETTES OF A PERSON HOLDING A TEST TUBE SYMBOLIZE SCIENCE. AMERICAN BANK NOTE'S ALONZO FORINGER ENGRAVED AT LEAST NINE SUCH VIGNETTES. COURTESY AMERICAN BANK NOTE COMPANY.

The Spanish-American War raised American spirits quite well, along with profit levels for such meat packers as Swift and such gun makers as Colt. It took plenty of protein to charge up San Juan Hill, and just as in the Civil War, the merchants of grain, meat, and eggs found the military a lucrative market. Thanks to Libby McNeil & Libby's canning methods, the nation's meat packers were feeding the U.S. troops compressed beef. The refrigerated rail car, though hardly more than a crude icebox on wheels, had transformed regional meat packers into national purveyors of animal parts, with satellite plants around the country and markets for their dressed beef in England, France, and Germany.

Back home a New Yorker could feast royally on veal chops and fritters at a cost of twenty-five cents and wash it down with a two-cent cup of coffee. And on America's big-city streets machines had begun to compete with the horse and buggy. Called motorcars, they were fashioned after low-tech bicycle technology and built by carriage and wagon makers, bicycle mechanics, and tinkerers. They included the gasoline-powered 1893 Duryea, 1894 Haynes, and 1898 Winton; the electric-powered 1898 Columbia and the 1901 steam-propelled White. The Columbia, Winton, and White made it into production thanks to the backing of investors. Such innovation was a fitting end to the Gay Nineties. By 1910, there would be sixty companies making automobiles with Henry Ford leading the pack with his Model T. Great distances, the building of roads, and the emergence of a prosperous middle class helped create the special relationship between Americans and their cars that continues to this day.

At the turn of the century there were 76 million Americans—one in three had been born in another country—most of them relying on horsepower and gaslight. Yet the United States was a mighty industrial power, leading the other industrialized nations in steel and textile production. The railroad was still the queen of transportation; one-third of all the railroad track in the world was in the United States. Along with the flow of goods, America's creative juices were also flowing in the early part of the century. The telephone, light bulb, phonograph, airplane, moving picture machine, and Model T Ford were among the myriad inventions that would change the way people lived, worked, and relaxed. American ingenuity also went underground with the launching of New York City's first subway in 1904, the same year the United States began work on the Panama Canal under the prodding of Teddy Roosevelt, the first president to see the United States as a global power.

While Roosevelt was attacking the monopolies, the knees of the American economy buckled. He was being blamed for the financial panic that struck in the autumn of 1907. Production had expanded beyond the nation's capacity to consume. The lull could have been withstood if the nation's banking and monetary systems had been stronger and if speculation had not been excessive. Panic set in after rumors of financial problems at Knickerbocker Trust, a leading New York bank, triggered a citywide run on the bank. Runs began on banks in New York and others failed, too. The panic was stemmed almost singlehandedly by

UNITED STATES LINES COMPANY

INCORPORATED UNDER THE LAWS OF THE STATE OF NEW JERSEY.
THIS CERTIFICATE IS TRANSFERABLE IN THE CITY OF NEW YORK OR IN HOBOKEN, N.J.

Number NC19556

Shares 100

This Certifies that —VINCENT ASTOR—

is the owner of ONE HUNDRED full paid and non-assessable shares OF THE COMMON STOCK OF THE PAR VALUE OF $1.00 EACH of United States Lines Company transferable on the books of the Corporation by the holder hereof in person or by duly authorized attorney upon surrender of this certificate properly endorsed. A statement of the powers, preferences and relative, participating, optional or other special rights of the Preferred Stock and of the Common Stock which the corporation is authorized to issue and of the qualifications, limitations or restrictions of such rights is printed upon the reverse hereof and this Certificate and the shares represented hereby are issued and shall be held subject to all the provisions of the Certificate of Organization of the corporation and of the amendments thereto (copies of which are on file with the Transfer Agent) to all of which the holder by acceptance hereof assents. This certificate is not valid unless countersigned by the Transfer Agent and registered by the Registrar.

Witness the seal of the Corporation and the facsimile signatures of its duly authorized officers.

Dated NOV 4 – 1949

TREASURER

PRESIDENT

UNITED STATES LINES COMPANY

ABOVE: After buying up banks, railroads and steel companies, J. Pierpont Morgan in 1902 formed the International Mercantile Company—the first international shipping cartel of its kind—with a fleet of ships that included the ill-fated *Titanic*. Among the companies Morgan acquired was the United States Lines, which was the first major shipping company to fly the American flag. The vignette, titled *Aviation No. 9* (1949), was drawn and engraved by Alonzo Foringer, premier artist for American Bank Note. Courtesy of George LaBarre.

Duesenberg Automobile & Motors Co., Inc.

100 SHARES

Number
12673

Shares
100

The Studebaker Corporation

FIRST STUDEBAKER SHOP

INCORPORATED UNDER THE LAWS OF THE STATE OF DELAWARE.

This Certifies that *Fritz E Harris*

is the owner of ONE HUNDRED fully paid and

non-assessable shares OF THE PAR VALUE OF ONE DOLLAR EACH OF THE COMMON STOCK of The Studebaker Corporation, a Delaware corporation, transferable on the books of the Corporation by said owner in person or by duly authorized attorney, upon surrender of this certificate properly endorsed. This certificate is not valid until countersigned by the Transfer Agent and registered by the Registrar. In Witness Whereof, the Corporation has caused the facsimile signatures of its proper officers, and its facsimile seal to be hereunto affixed.

COMMON

Dated: MAR 14 1935

The Studebaker Corporation

By *Paul G. Hoffman*
PRESIDENT.

SECRETARY.

REGISTERED:
THE COMMERCIAL NATIONAL BANK AND TRUST COMPANY,
OF NEW YORK, REGISTRAR.
By

AUTHORIZED OFFICER.

COUNTERSIGNED:
THE MARINE MIDLAND TRUST COMPANY
OF NEW YORK,
TRANSFER AGENT.
By

ASSISTANT SECRETARY.

AMERICAN BANK NOTE COMPANY.

THE STUDEBAKER CORPORATION

ABOVE: STUDEBAKER HAS AN INTERESTING HISTORY THAT BEGAN WHEN THE STUDEBAKER BROTHERS OPENED A BLACKSMITH AND WAGON-BUILDING SHOP, THE SUBJECT OF THE HIGHLY DETAILED CENTER VIGNETTE IN THIS SHARE, CIRCA 1935. LATER AN AUTOMOBILE MANUFACTURER, THE COMPANY'S FIRST CAR WAS INTRODUCED IN 1902 AND BROKE STOCK CAR RECORDS WITH OUTSTANDING PERFORMANCE. COURTESY OF GEORGE HEWITSON COLLECTIBLES.

SHARES $100 EACH

ED STOCK

FIRS

ED STATES WORSTED CORPOR

C 152

RED STOCK

PAR VALUE $100 EACH.

COMMO

240,000 SHARE

OMPTON & KNOWLES LOOM WO

INCORPORATED UNDER THE LAWS OF

ARIZONA

No. 71

Shares — 300 —

Oklahoma Oil Corporation

SHARES 5,000,000   PAR VALUE $1.00

Capital Stock $5,000,000.00

THIS CERTIFIES THAT *C. A. Winter* is the owner of

Three Hundred Shares of the Capital Stock of

Oklahoma Oil Corporation, *fully paid and non-assessable*

transferable only on the books of the Corporation by the holder

hereof in person or by Attorney, upon surrender of this Certificate

properly endorsed.

In Witness Whereof, *the said Corporation has caused this Certificate to be*

signed by its duly authorized officers and to be sealed with the Seal of the Corporation

this 24th day of June A.D. 1921

SECRETARY

J. Paul Getty

PRESIDENT

SHARES $1.00   EACH

© GOES 59

OKLAHOMA OIL CORPORATION

ABOVE: OKLAHOMA OIL CORPORATION WAS JUST THE BEGINNING OF WHAT SOMEDAY WOULD GROW INTO THE GETTY OIL COMPANY, THE MASTER LINK IN JOHN PAUL GETTY'S HOLDINGS AND THE WORLD'S LARGEST PERSONALLY CONTROLLED OIL COMPANY. THE VIGNETTES ALONG THE BORDER OF THIS STOCK (CIRCA 1921) TELL THE STORY OF OIL PRODUCTION AND IRONICALLY DEPICT HOW SOMEDAY GETTY WOULD INTEGRATE AND CONTROL ALL ASPECTS OF OIL OPERATIONS: EXPLORING, REFINING, STORING, AND TRANSPORTING. COURTESY OF GEORGE LABARRE.

J. P. Morgan, Sr., who orchestrated a massive operation to infuse cash into banks and shore up the stock market. In Chicago, banks also faced a currency famine as people hoarded cash out of fear that the banks wouldn't honor checks. Roosevelt condemned the "speculation, corruption, and fraud" that fueled the panic, and he sought financial reforms that would strengthen the nation's banking system.

It took six years before the monetary system was taken out of the grip of the J. P. Morgans and put in the hands of the federal government with the passage of the Federal Reserve Act of 1913. By then Woodrow Wilson was president. Setting up the Federal Reserve Board and the regional Reserve Banks was considered the most important statute of Wilson's administration. He gave the nation its first efficient banking system since Andrew Jackson's term, and more reform followed a year later in a bill drafted by Louis Brandeis to create the Federal Trade Commission, which was established to prevent the unlawful suppression of competition. Other economic reforms were being considered, but were shelved along with America's isolationism as the nation went to war.

Shortly after America entered World War I in the spring of 1917, both wages and prices began to rise sharply. Congress granted Wilson broad wartime mobilization powers, which authorized him to set the prices of many commodities and to regulate factories and transportation facilities. The American War Industries Board controlled manufacturing and the Food Administration was responsible for civilian and military supply. The government had halted antitrust suits during the war, but price competition

was narrowed as well. Nevertheless, both labor and the farmers shared extensively in wartime prosperity. The orgy of production sent prices up rapidly, but wages climbed at a faster rate. Demand for commodities from apples to zinc was strong, and prices continued to rise after the armistice was signed on November 11, 1918, pushing American unions to resort to strikes. In 1919 alone there were more than 3,600 strikes across the nation.

On the world front, an idealistic Wilson was trying to forge a plan for future peace through the League of Nations. At home, his administration continued to impose wartime controls in an effort to keep a lid on prices, while the postwar politicians promised that prosperity was on its way. The consumer, economists kept insisting, would be the savior of private enterprise in America, even though profits from the bushel of corn the farmer sold could buy five gallons of gasoline in 1919 and only bought half a gallon in 1920.

Around the corner another era unfolded with different fads, changing morals, and a new wave of materialism. The 1920s were a time of prosperity, normalcy, Warren G. Harding, Calvin Coolidge, and Herbert Hoover. Movies and radio were beginning to take shape and, despite the national Prohibition Act against the use of alcohol, liquor flowed illegally from so-called speakeasies where people drank while they swayed to the strains of a new musical sound called jazz that had filtered north from New Orleans. The author F. Scott Fitzgerald called this era the Jazz Age, and eloquently captured it in his 1925 classic *The Great Gatsby*. During the decade there would be a 400 percent increase in millionaires

National its biscuits. "We grew up founding our dreams on the infinite promises of American advertising," said Zelda Fitzgerald, the wife of F. Scott Fitzgerald. "I still believe that one can learn to play the piano by mail and that mud will give you a perfect complexion."

Even Calvin Coolidge had acknowledged advertising's power, calling the rising phenomenon "the most potent influence in adopting and changing the habits and modes of life—affecting what we eat, what we wear, and the work and play of a whole nation." Consumers were showered with premiums, prizes, and gifts for their patronage, along with reduced down payments, generous credit terms, and trade-in allowances. The public relations man emerged in corporate America as a Mr. Fix-It for whom no detail was too trivial when it came to influencing the public favorably or unfavorably.

LEFT: VIEWING THE BORDER OF MOBIL OIL'S CERTIFICATE (1966) IS LIKE LOOKING THROUGH A KALEIDOSCOPE. THE GEOMETRIC LATHE HAD TO WORK OVERTIME TO PRODUCE THESE COMPLEX DESIGNS. PEGASUS WAS ENGRAVED BY JOSEPH KELLER FOR AMERICAN BANK NOTE. COURTESY GEORGE LABARRE.

over the previous decade and for the first time, in 1920, more Americans lived in urban centers than in rural towns. That's where the jobs were. Now it took fewer farmers to grow more food because technology had revolutionized the farm. In 1918 there were 80,000 tractors; in 1929 there were 850,000.

Manufacturers were giddy over their prospects of opening new markets for their products. In 1920, for every hundred Americans there were only thirteen bathtubs and six telephones. One American family in every three had an automobile and one in ten thousand had a radio. And only one in every ten city homes was wired for electricity. By now advertising had come into its own. Cadillac was advertising its "runabouts," Camel its cigarettes, Atlantic its gasoline, and

Hoover tried to give the nation a businesslike government with little idealistic promise. He had emerged from wartime service with a grand scheme he pushed, first as secretary of commerce, and then as president: an alliance between the federal government, trade associations, and the giant corporations. The result boosted the number of trade associations from a dozen in 1920 to more than two thousand when Hoover left the White House in 1932. Hoover's call to rugged individualism had been pushed aside somewhere in his pragmatic engineer's mind. Federal activity in economic affairs under Republican administration had coiled back in the 1920s, allowing big corporations to grow, on the average, three times as fast as smaller ones. Such concerns as Kroger Company, for example, grew through vertical integration, buying up bakeries, packing houses, and coffee-roasting plants. The big meat packers like Swift and Wilson bought ranches to raise their own cattle and farms for chickens and eggs.

All the while American farmers and industrialists grew fearful of being inundated with cheap produce and products from depressed European labor. A Republican Congress became protection-minded and in the spring of 1921 rushed to passage an "emergency" tariff bill, which outgoing President Wilson vetoed, arguing, "If there ever was a time when America had anything to fear from foreign competition that time has passed."

The following year, Congress passed the Fordney-McCumber Act, a tariff law that set the highest rates in U.S. history up to that time, and protectionism was in full bloom. The act authorized the president to raise or lower duties by as much as 50 percent if recommended by the Tariff Commission (Warren Harding and his successor Calvin Coolidge used the provision thirty-seven times, twenty-one of which increased tariffs on such commodities as pig iron, chemicals, butter, and cheese.) The predictable result was a tariff war that cut deeply into the United States's foreign trade. It was the tariffs of the 1920s that a number of today's economists think sparked the Great Depression. Maybe so—

but prosperity during the Roaring Twenties bulled ahead in spite of the tariffs rather than because of them, and few could argue against prosperity.

Especially the speculators. In Boston a charming fellow named Charles Ponzi schemed to put pyramid deals together. The deals were the classic investment fraud in which the operator pays high returns to current investors from the money of new investors. Since the money was never invested in any land, to keep the scam going Ponzi had to attract more and more investors. Meanwhile, real estate sharks in Florida sold unwary investors thousands of acres of swampy land, which led to economic bust. Economist John Kenneth Galbraith in *The Great Crash* described the Florida boom as "...the first indication of the mood of the twenties and the conviction that God intended the middle class to be rich." Newspapers and popular periodicals of the day ran all sorts of "how to" stories that bolstered the notion that wealth was in everyone's destiny. Typical of such articles was one in *Ladies' Home Journal* titled "Everyone Ought to Be Rich," which laid out a twenty-year investment plan in common stocks. The article had been written by John H. Raskob, one of Wall Street's major bullish speculators.

The speculative frenzy in real estate, insurance, and commodities spilled over into Wall Street where tips, rumors, and hearsay spun the stock market like a top—similar thorns that had pricked the South Sea Bubble two hundred years earlier. In 1923, some 236 million shares of stock were traded annually on the New York Stock Exchange. By 1928,

INCORPORATED UNDER THE LAWS

THE HOBOKEN

CA

NUMBER

A130

189

TRUST COMPANY REGISTRAR

SEPARATARY

THIS CERTIFIES that

is entitled to Forty

CAPITAL STOCK $3,300,000.

INCORPORATED UNDER THE LAWS OF THE STATE OF NEW JERSEY.

THE HOBOKEN FERRY COMPANY

FULL PAID CAPITAL STOCK.

ISSUED FOR PROPERTY PURCHASED.

NUMBER
A130

SHARES
40

THIS CERTIFIES that D. G. M. Johnson is entitled to Forty Shares fully paid, in the Capital Stock of The Hoboken Ferry Company, transferable only on the books of the Company in person or by attorney on surrender of this certificate. In Witness Whereof the said Company has caused its corporate seal to be affixed hereto and this certificate to be signed by its President and Treasurer this day of Feb 1897.

COUNTERSIGNED AND REGISTERED
FEB 8 1897
UNITED STATES MORTGAGE & TRUST COMPANY
REGISTRAR

TREASURER.

Emanuel Lehman PRESIDENT.

SHARES $100 EACH.

THE HOMER LEE BANK NOTE CO. NEW YORK.

THE HOBOKEN FERRY COMPANY

OPPOSITE AND ABOVE: HOBOKEN (THE ALGONKIAN WORD FOR TOBACCO PIPE) NEW JERSEY, ACROSS THE HUDSON RIVER FROM LOWER MANHATTAN, HAS A MILE-LONG WATERFRONT WITH PIERS SERVING BOTH PASSENGER AND FREIGHT STEAMSHIP LINES. THE FERRY TRAFFIC HAS BEEN ACTIVE SINCE THE SEVENTEENTH CENTURY. THIS CERTIFICATE (1897) WITH ITS STRONG GRAPHICS AND SCULPTED BORDERS (PRINTED BY THE HOMER BANK NOTE COMPANY), IS A FINE EXAMPLE OF THE GOLDEN ERA OF ENGRAVED PRINTING THAT DOMINATED THE 1880S AND 1890S. COURTESY GEORGE LABARRE.

OPPOSITE: VARIATIONS ON THE SAME ALLEGORICAL THEME, *WINGED MAN & WOMAN*, ORIGINATED FOR REO MOTOR CAR IN 1916. COURTESY R. M. SMYTHE & CO., INC. (TOP AND BOTTOM) AND DAVID BEACH (CENTER).

1.125 billion shares changed hands in the year. By then, concludes William E. Leuchtenburg in *Perils of Prosperity 1914–1932,* "The stock market was carrying the whole economy." He adds: "If it had not been for the wave of speculation, the prosperity of the twenties might have ended much earlier than it did."

Among the heavily traded stocks were General Motors (GM) and Radio Corporation of America (RCA). Investors who had bought General Motors at $99 a share in 1925 were sitting with GM stock worth $212 a share in 1928. And the stock was moving higher, driven by the big speculators, notably W. C. Durant, Arthur Cutten, the Fisher Brothers, and John Raskob. GM was attractive for fundamental reasons. Ford, still a private company, had shut down in 1927 to retool, for the Model A. General Motors (and other auto makers) took advantage of the situation by increasing production and sales. The momentum allowed GM to surpass Ford to become the leading auto producer in the industry. When GM released its annual report in February 1928, its stock proved irresistible. It helped, too, that GM's president predicted a rise in the stock price from 180 to 225, along with the promise to return to stockholders 60 percent of the company's earnings.

RCA, the other favorite, was in the forefront of radio production, transmission, and other electronic technologies. Its sales had jumped from $5.8 million in 1925 to $7.4 million in 1926. By March 1928 sales had climbed to $11.8 million and the company was engaged in merger talks with its largest customer, Victor Talking Machine. Its prospects for future growth looked rosy and were being touted by Robert Sarnoff, RCA's founder and CEO. Sarnoff got his start in the electronics industry with the American Marconi Company as a wireless operator who picked up the dots and dashes from the *Carpathian* as it was steaming to rescue the doomed *Titanic* in 1912. Like GM, RCA had become big and important enough to be included in the Dow Jones Industrial Average when it first appeared with thirty stocks on October 1, 1928. But unlike GM's promise of higher dividends to its shareholders, RCA made no such promise for a simple reason. It paid no dividends, nor would it for years to come.

RCA wasn't the only heavily traded stock that paid no dividends. Others that did not pay but were widely held included Radio-Keith-Orpheum (RKO), the motion picture company; Aluminum Company of America; and the United Aircraft and Transport Corporation. Many of the public utility holding companies paid no dividends either. Among them were Commonwealth and Southern Corporation, Electric Bond and Share, and the North American Company. Actually the demand in utility stocks outpaced that of the industrial stocks, while the railroad stocks simply languished. The high demand in utility stock showed a willing public eager to buy shares in new industries. Of the popular public utility stocks, Eugene White in *Crashes And Panics* writes: "This was another frontier industry with potentially high but uncertain returns.

SHELL OIL COMPANY

REO MOTOR CAR COMPANY

SHARES $10 EACH

INCORPORATED UNDER THE LAWS   OF THE STATE OF DELAWARE.

DURANT MOTORS, INCORPORATED.

GENERAL ELECTRIC COMPANY

COMMON STOCK
$5 PAR VALUE

COMMON STOCK
$5 PAR VALUE

NY/G 597025

10

INCORPORATED UNDER THE LAWS OF THE STATE OF NEW YORK.

GENERAL ELECTRIC COMPANY

THIS CERTIFICATE MAY BE PRESENTED FOR TRANSFER EITHER IN NEW YORK CITY, IN BOSTON, OR IN TORONTO, CANADA.

This Certifies That CLARENCE M. GREGG★★★ is the owner of

★ ★ ★ ★ TEN ★ ★ ★ ★

FULL-PAID AND NON-ASSESSABLE SHARES OF THE PAR VALUE OF $5 EACH OF THE COMMON STOCK

of General Electric Company transferable in person or by duly authorized attorney on the books of the Company upon surrender of this certificate properly endorsed. This Certificate is not valid until countersigned by the Transfer Agent and registered by the Registrar. Witness the seal of the Company and the signatures of its duly authorized officers.

Dated DEC -6 1957

John D. Lockton
TREASURER

Ralph J. Cordiner
PRESIDENT

TRUST COMPANY OF NEW YORK, REGISTRAR

AUTHORIZED OFFICER.

COUNTERSIGNED: GENERAL ELECTRIC COMPANY, (NEW YORK, N.Y.)

TRANSFER AGENT.

AMERICAN BANK NOTE COMPANY.

GENERAL ELECTRIC COMPANY

ABOVE: GENERAL ELECTRIC WAS FORMED IN 1892 THROUGH THE MERGER OF THOMSON-HOUSTON COMPANY AND EDISON ELECTRIC COMPANY, FOUNDED BY THOMAS EDISON IN 1878. BY 1895, GE WAS BUILDING THE WORLD'S LARGEST ELECTRIC LOCOMOTIVES AND TRANSFORMERS. IN 1954 IT BUILT THE FIRST JET ENGINE THAT MOVED AT TWICE THE SPEED OF SOUND AS IT CONTINUED TO MAKE WASHING MACHINES AND TOASTER OVENS. DURING THE 1980s, GE RESTRUCTURED ITSELF TO MEET GLOBAL COMPETITION AND BOUGHT RADIO CORPORATION OF AMERICA, WHICH INCLUDED THE NBC NETWORK. TODAY THE MARKET VALUE OF ITS STOCK EXCEEDS $200 BILLION. COURTESY OF R.M. SMYTH & CO., INC.

Like the firms in manufacturing, these utilities' rapid growth, short histories, and lack of a dividend record made them easy favorites in a speculative way."

The intensity of an untethered economy tied to a boom psychology ended in the 1929 stock market plunge that sent the nation spinning into darkness. Men and women in the offices of their stockbrokers hunched over inverted glass bowls watching clattering spools of ticker tape stamped with cryptic numerals unwind along with their lives. In early October, RCA plunged 32 points, General Electric dropped 50 points, and U.S. Steel fell nearly 60 points. The market rallied for a brief period, but on Thursday, October 24, it broke violently downward, wiping out months, and even years, of gains in a matter of hours. Over the next few days U.S. Steel lost another 17 1/2 points, Westinghouse, 34 1/2, G.E. 47 1/2, and RCA, 22. The drastic drops were reflected in the Dow Jones Industrial Average. In September 1929 the Dow stood at 452. By November it had slipped 50 percent to 224. On July 8, 1932, in the grip of the depression, the Dow would sink to a startling 58. In three years General Motors had dropped from 73 to 8, U.S. Steel from 262 to 22, Montgomery Ward from 138 to 4, and RCA from 114 to 2.

Politically and economically everything had gone wrong. Nobody seemed to be calling the shots. Responsibility was diffused in a society that had grown stubborn, greedy, and, some would say, self-destructive. At the time not everyone in the stock market had bought on margin—the use of borrowed money from brokerage firms to buy stock—although it seemed that way. (A Senate committee in the wake of the crash esti-mated that only 1.5 million out of a population of 120 million had been active in the market in 1929. And most of the investors, contrary to popular belief, were cash customers.) But there had been enough buyers, representing every social strata in America. In his classic history *Only Yesterday* Frederick Lewis Allen colorfully captured the fever of the players: "The rich man's chauffeur drove with his ears laid back to catch the news of an impending move in Bethlehem Steel; he held fifty shares himself on a twenty-point margin. The window-cleaner at the broker's office paused to watch the ticker, for he was thinking of converting his laboriously accumulated savings into a few shares of Simmons. Edwin Lefevre (an articulate reporter on the market at this time who could claim considerable personal experience) told of a broker's valet who made nearly a quarter of a million in the market, of a trained nurse who cleaned up thirty thousand following the tips given her by grateful patients; and of a Wyoming cattleman, thirty miles from the nearest railroad, who bought or sold a thousand shares a day."

It doesn't sound all that different from current market participants. Stock fever, it seems, has gripped everyone from the Des Moines dentist to the New York psychoanalyst, from the Miami construction worker to the Lost Angeles barber, the same bunch that in the late 1960s and 1970s had its favorite high-flying stock, one that sold at a multiple of 100 to 200 times earnings projected years in the future. Now, cell phone in hand, they bark orders to their brokers chasing after the high-tech stocks with bio, micro, net, or computer in their names. And more and more are bypassing brokers to trade through the Internet.

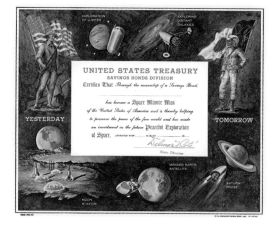

But the economy of the twenties was far different from today's. Back then on the surface everything appeared healthy. National income was high and unemployment low during the decade. But there was a flaw in the economic timber: Most of the wealth was in the hands of a few. In 1920, for every one hundred people in American cities, one house in every ten city homes was wired for electricity. Only one in ten thousand had a radio. Nearly one-third of the country's breadwinners earned less than $2,000 a year, and one-fifth less than $1,000. In the fall of 1929—when the stock market crashed—nearly four times as many employers reported increases in wages to the Bureau of Labor Statistics as wage reductions. A year later the situation was reversed. And getting worse. In 1931, derelicts sleeping in parks and long lines of unemployed were images of an urban nightmare that had never before existed. Oranges were a dime a dozen; lamb chops were twelve cents a pound; eggs were eight cents a dozen—all good buys, if you could afford them. Fewer and fewer could. Ironically, the fount of Democratic capitalism had come to suggest not a wellspring of wealth and growth, but a cesspool of poverty and stagnation. All this happened amid farm surpluses and lack of any mechanism to maintain prices. The nation had slipped into a kind of dreamy trance, and the tableau of soup line, and street-corner apple hawkers was ineffably sad. The president's name had become synonymous with the deplorable conditions: Tarpaper shacks that had sprung up like weeds on vacant lots were called Hoovervilles, newspapers were "Hoover blankets," and empty pockets, "Hoover flags." Even nature turned against humankind as droughts and dust storms afflicted the farm belt, forcing tens of thousands of ruined farmers to pack up their families in old jalopies and flee to what they hoped was the "promised land" in California.

All this in the lap of industrial progress. By 1932, America's industrialization had essentially been complete, contends Leuchtenburg in *The Perils of Prosperity.* "Machines," he writes, "had replaced the old artisans; there were few coopers, blacksmiths, or cobblers left. The livery stable had been torn down to make way for the filling station....The Old West had disappeared....The empire builders like James Hill (developer of the Great Northern Railway in the 1890s) were gone....The metropolis had

ABOVE: AFTER WORLD WAR II THE U.S. TREASURY STARTED SENDING "THANK YOU" CERTIFICATES TO AMERICANS WHO HAD BOUGHT GOVERNMENT BONDS. THE CERTIFICATES FEATURED DISNEY CHARACTERS IN THE 1940S; L'IL ABNER IN THE 1950S; AND SPACE EXPLORATION IN THE 1970S. COURTESY OF GEORGE LABARRE.

ABOVE: MEDALLIONS AT THE UPPER CORNERS OF STOCK CERTIFICATES CAME IN ALL SIZES, SHAPES, AND DESIGNS. THEY GENERALLY INDICATED THE NUMBER OF SHARES OR THE CERTIFICATE'S SERIAL NUMBER. AND BECAUSE OF THEIR INTRICATE DESIGNS, THEY WERE A WAY TO FOIL COUNTERFEITING ATTEMPTS. THEY WERE ENGRAVED WITH PARALLEL LINES, CROSSING LINES, AND SCROLLS WITH BORDERS THAT BLENDED IN WITH THE CERTIFICATE. THE WORK TO PRODUCE THESE SMALL FEATURES WAS TEDIOUS AND TIME-CONSUMING, LIKE THAT OF ENGRAVING THE VIGNETTE ITSELF, WHICH COULD TAKE WEEKS OR MONTHS TO FINISH. ONCE COMPLETED, HOWEVER, THEY BECAME CHOICES ON A SPECIMEN SHEET FOR REPEATED USE.

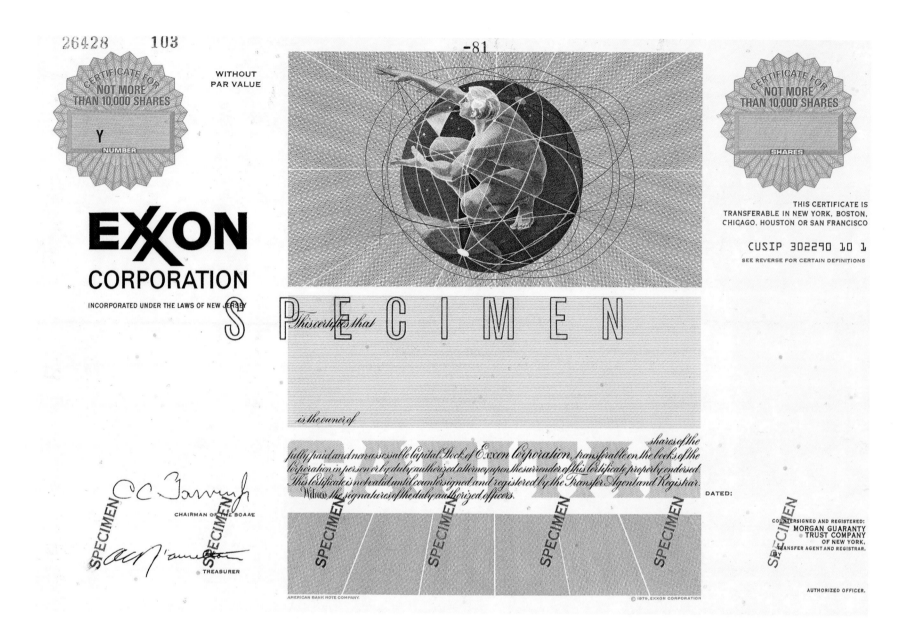

26428 103

-81

CERTIFICATE FOR
NOT MORE
THAN 10,000 SHARES

Y
NUMBER

WITHOUT
PAR VALUE

EXXON
CORPORATION

INCORPORATED UNDER THE LAWS OF NEW JERSEY

SPECIMEN

This certifies that

is the owner of

fully paid and non-assessable Capital Stock of Exxon Corporation, transferable on the books of the Corporation in person or by duly authorized attorney upon the surrender of this Certificate properly endorsed This Certificate is not valid until countersigned and registered by the Transfer Agent and Registrar. Witness the signatures of the duly authorized officers.

CHAIRMAN OF THE BOARD

TREASURER

SPECIMEN   SPECIMEN   SPECIMEN   SPECIMEN

AMERICAN BANK NOTE COMPANY.

© 1979, EXXON CORPORATION

CERTIFICATE FOR
NOT MORE
THAN 10,000 SHARES

SHARES

THIS CERTIFICATE IS
TRANSFERABLE IN NEW YORK, BOSTON,
CHICAGO, HOUSTON OR SAN FRANCISCO

CUSIP 302290 10 1

SEE REVERSE FOR CERTAIN DEFINITIONS

DATED:

COUNTERSIGNED AND REGISTERED:
MORGAN GUARANTY
TRUST COMPANY
OF NEW YORK,
TRANSFER AGENT AND REGISTRAR,
BY

AUTHORIZED OFFICER.

EXXON CORPORATION

ABOVE: EXXON CORPORATION TRACES ITS ROOTS TO THE 1882 FOUNDING OF JOHN D. ROCKEFELLER'S STANDARD OIL COMPANY OF NEW JERSEY. BY 1950, IT WAS DOING BUSINESS IN 150 COUNTRIES, AND IN 1972 IT CHANGED ITS NAME FROM JERSEY STANDARD TO EXXON CORPORATION, SELECTED MAINLY FOR ITS DISTINCTIVENESS. A YEAR LATER, IT ABANDONED THE ESSO NAME UNDER WHICH IT HAD MARKETED ITS GAS WITH THE FAMOUS "PUT A TIGER IN YOUR TANK" SLOGAN, A MOVE AT THE TIME WHICH COST $100 MILLION. THE CUSTOMIZED VIGNETTE OF A MAN INSIDE SPHERES TITLED ENERGY WAS ENGRAVED BY KENNETH GUY FOR AMERICAN BANK NOTE COMPANY. COURTESY OF R.M. SMYTHE & CO., INC.

shattered the supremacy of the small town, and life seemed infinitely more impersonal."

In the presidential election of 1932, American voters threw out President Hoover and replaced him with Franklin Roosevelt, who earlier had flown to Chicago to accept his party's nomination. There he pledged "a new deal for the American people" to the cheers and strains of "Happy Days are Here Again." Thus, under a banner of acronyms, a string of agencies were created in Roosevelt's New Deal era—such agencies as the SEC (Securities & Exchange Commission), the TVA (Tennessee Valley Authority), the FDIC (Federal Deposit Insurance Commission), the CCC (Civil Conservation Corps), the REA (Rural Electrification Administration), and the NLRB (National Labor Relations Board). And the structure of the securities industry was set up with the passage of the Securities and Exchange Act, which regulated the practices of securities brokers, dealers, and exchanges, and the Glass-Steagall Act, which divided the commercial and investment banking industries into two distinct business segments.

It was crisis management by proxy. Big business hated Roosevelt with ferocity. The reason was obvious: They feared the New Dealers would trample the spirit of free enterprise so thoroughly that it would never recover, and the country would forever lapse from "New Deal to New Dole," as detractors put it. But Roosevelt wasn't out to remake or redefine a social and economic structure, only to adjust it. In essence, his role was more like that of a receiver in bankruptcy. The Roosevelt Administration had also embarked on a risky

course of replacing an open market with government management of agriculture. There were almost no precedents for such tricky devices as official price fixing, subsidies, and production controls.

As 1932 came to a close, American business had failed to respond to the low costs and low interest rates of the previous three years. The six million unemployed in 1930 had grown to sixteen million—25 percent of the work force—in 1933. The mechanics of the free market had failed to operate effectively in situations of limited competition and rigid price control. This caused the depression to linger as corporate America learned to cling to solvency by the tips of its financial fingers. By 1940, the old days of laissez-faire were gone, replaced by a new form of capitalism. Government had stepped in when private initiative faltered, to form a union. Although this seemed restrictive, it opened new frontiers of economic freedom.

The demands of World War II saved the day. Across the Atlantic, the Nazi menace had driven the British back to their island, and by the end of 1940, Hitler controlled most of western Europe, including France. Back in the United States the rumblings of war had grown louder. Four years later, on June 6, 1944, when news reached the United States that 176,000 assault troops stormed the Normandy beaches to free the French, Americans knew the worst was over. New corporate names vital to the war effort had flashed across the stock ticker: Boeing, Northrup, Chance Vought, Hughes, Pratt & Whitney, Sikorsky, Curtiss, Douglas, and McDonnell were a few of them.

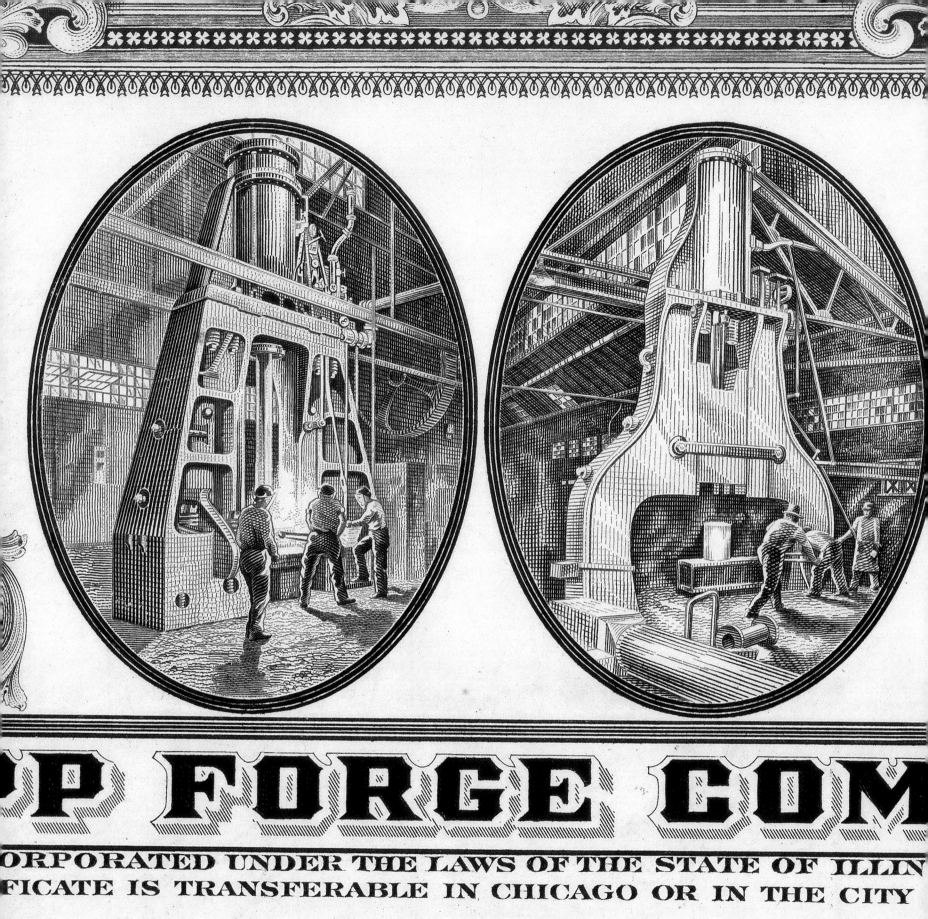

P FORGE COM

ROY A. KROPP

The American economy had thrived on war. During the period from 1940 to 1945, the gross national product more than doubled to $215.2 billion, while the cost of living remained stable, due to tight price controls and rationing. Weekly earnings in 1950 were pumped up to nearly twice their 1944 level and Americans itched to spend money on homes, cars, refrigerators, steaks, bacon, butter, sugar, coffee, chocolate, chewing gum, nylons, shoes, gasoline—anything and everything that was scarce during the war. Savings were high, and demand went up.

POSTWAR PROSPERITY

There was promise in an economy that was converting its guns back to butter as the wartime production boom was being replaced by an insatiable demand for merchandise. Consumers stormed a new beachhead—department stores, where sales reached a postwar peak of thirty billion dollars in 1948, nearly triple what they had been in 1940.

The nation's industrialists focused their concern on how to adjust to a postwar era that would suddenly be without life-sustaining government largess. Many remembered the sting of an economy that fell with a thud following demobilization after World War I. Back then the price controls chief, Bernard M. Baruch, simply resigned the day after the armistice. Economists bemoaned the fact that such cavalier planning had delayed orderly peacetime conversion by more than two years.

About a month after President Roosevelt died, victory in Europe came. Then on August 14, 1945, the Japanese surrendered and within a few hours people were pasting their rationing coupons into their memory books. Two days later the Army sent manufacturers some sixty thousand form telegrams canceling contracts worth $7.3 billion, and the giant industrial machine that helped to reshape the world's geopolitical face began to be dismantled.

The scramble for income alternatives was pandemic. The industrial renaissance had left a crop of factories loaded

OPPOSITE: KROPP FORGE COMPANY MADE MOLDED METAL PRODUCTS CALLED CASTINGS. THE PROCESS OF POURING MELTED METALS IS CALLED FOUNDING. THE CERTIFICATE'S VIGNETTE (SHOWN HERE FROM 1954), ENGRAVED BY AMERICAN BANK NOTE COMPANY, IS CUSTOMIZED. COURTESY OF GEORGE LABARRE.

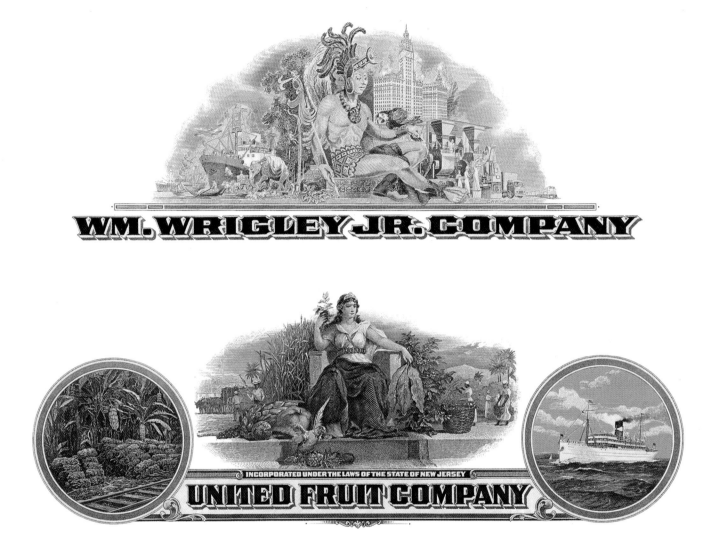

with the latest tools and machinery ready to produce for a peacetime economy. In Chicago, for example, there were 9,058 manufacturing firms when the war began and more than 12,000 when it ended. Chrysler switched its tank production back to cars, while Kaiser converted its shipyard to an automobile factory. Ford converted its Tri-Motor plane and propeller production back to cars and trucks. Motorola, which made walkie-talkies, began to turn out radios and television sets. Smaller outfits that made time fuses used in anti-aircraft shells went back to making watches. Steel used in the massive war machine was now being molded for bridges and buildings by many companies, including U.S. Steel, Bethlehem, Jones & Laughlin, and Inland. A flock of companies began manufacturing consumer products made of a newfangled material called plastic.

The big question that had politicians and economists

ABOVE: WRIGLEY'S VIGNETTE FEATURES THE CITY OF CHICAGO, WHERE THE CHEWING GUM PRODUCER IS BASED. UNITED FRUIT'S CENTER VIGNETTE IS CALLED *AGRICULTURE*. COURTESY GEORGE LABARRE (TOP) AND STOCK SEARCH INTERNATIONAL (BOTTOM).

COMMON STOCK   COMMON STOCK

CERTIFICATE FOR LESS THAN 100 SHARES

Number
074551

Shares
50

INCORPORATED UNDER THE LAWS   OF THE STATE OF NEW YORK.

GIMBEL BROTHERS, INC.

BY

EDWARD P. BLACK,

This Certifies that

is the owner of   FIFTY   fully paid and non-assessable shares, WITHOUT NOMINAL OR PAR VALUE OF THE COMMON STOCK of Gimbel Brothers, Inc (hereinafter called the "Company"), transferable on the books of the Company by the holder hereof in person or by duly authorized attorney upon surrender of this certificate properly endorsed. A statement of the rights, privileges, preferences and voting powers and of the restrictions or qualifications of the $6 Cumulative Preferred Stock and of the Common Stock of the Company is printed upon the back hereof, and this Certificate and the shares represented hereby are issued and shall be subject to all of the provisions of the Certificate of Incorporation of the Company (a copy of which is on file at the office of the Transfer Agent), to all of which the holder, by the acceptance hereof, assents. This certificate is not valid unless countersigned by the Transfer Agent and registered by the Registrar.

In Witness Whereof, Gimbel Brothers, Inc. has caused this certificate to be signed by its proper officers and its corporate seal to be hereunto affixed. Dated JAN 25 1946

REGISTERED:
The COMMERCIAL NATIONAL BANK AND TRUST COMPANY OF NEW YORK
By AUTHORIZED OFFICER.

COUNTERSIGNED
GUARANTY TRUST COMPANY OF NEW YORK.
AS TRANSFER AGENT.
AUTHORIZED OFFICER.

JAN 25 1946

Samuel Nass
TREASURER.

Bernard F. Gimbel
PRESIDENT.

SHARES WITHOUT PAR VALUE

GIMBEL BROTHERS INC
NEW YORK
1922

FULL PAID AND NON ASSESSABLE

AMERICAN BANK NOTE COMPANY.

TENS UNITS
1 1
2 2
3 3
4 4
5 5
6 6
7 7
8 8
9 9
0 0
SHARES

GIMBEL BROTHERS, INC.

ABOVE: THE RETAIL WAR BETWEEN NEW YORK DEPARTMENT STORES GIMBEL BROTHERS AND MACY'S WAS LEGENDARY. ORIGINALLY AN INDIANA TRADING POST DATING FROM 1842, THE GIMBEL BROTHERS OPENED THEIR NEW YORK STORE ON HERALD SQUARE—A BLOCK FROM MACY'S—IN 1910, AND THE WAR BEGAN. IF LOCATION WAS EVERYTHING, SO WAS PRICE. GIMBELS INVENTED THE BARGAIN BASEMENT. IN 1922, GIMBELS ACQUIRED SAKS & COMPANY AND OPENED SAKS FIFTH AVENUE IN 1924. THE CERTIFICATE'S VIGNETTE (1948) WAS ENGRAVED BY ALFRED JONES, FORMER HEAD OF AMERICAN BANK NOTE'S PICTURE DEPARTMENT. COURTESY OF GEORGE LABARRE.

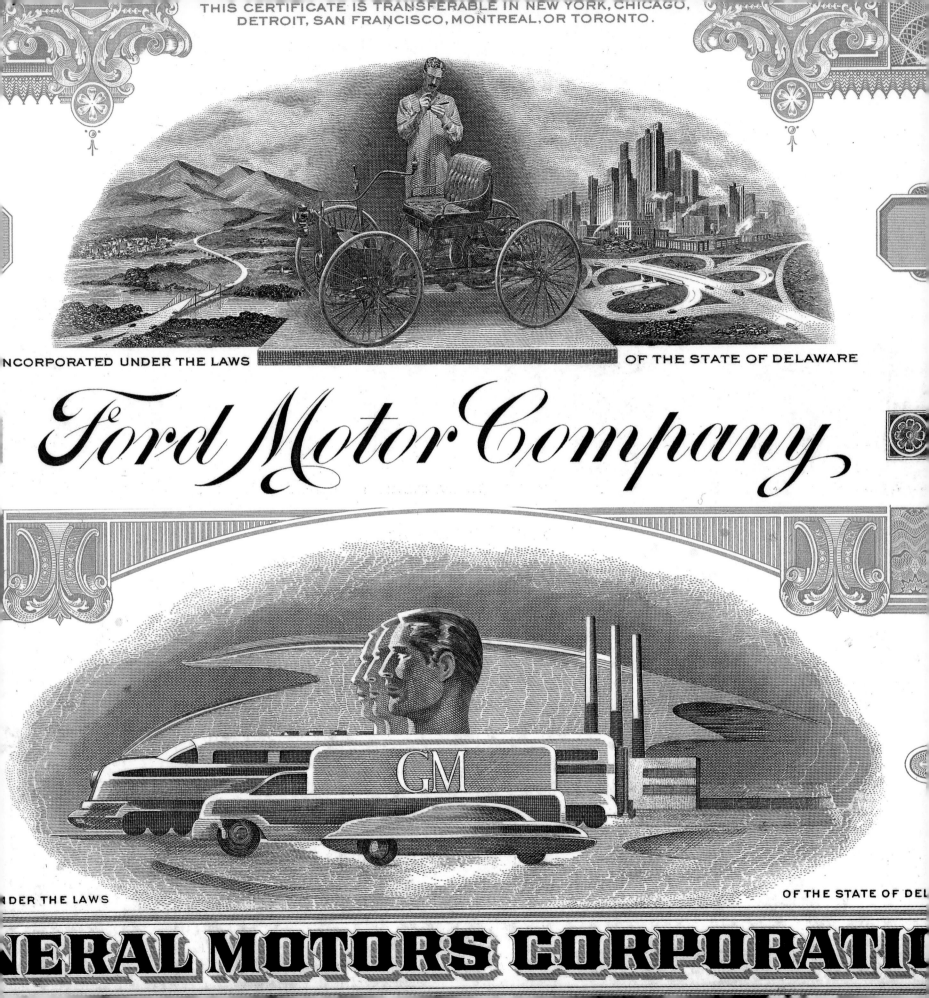

THIS CERTIFICATE IS TRANSFERABLE IN NEW YORK, CHICAGO, DETROIT, SAN FRANCISCO, MONTREAL, OR TORONTO.

INCORPORATED UNDER THE LAWS OF THE STATE OF DELAWARE

Ford Motor Company

GM

NDER THE LAWS OF THE STATE OF DEL

NERAL MOTORS CORPORATIO

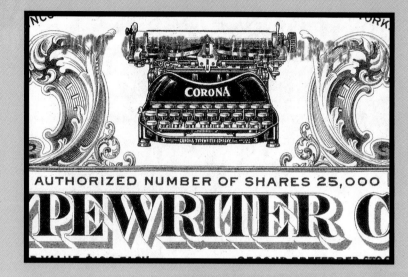

ABOVE: FOR MANY SHAREHOLDERS, THE VIGNETTE THAT RENDERED A COMPANY'S PRODUCT WAS AS CLOSE AS THEY CAME TO SEEING THEIR INVESTMENT. (UPPER LEFT) L.C. SMITH & CORONA TYPEWRITERS INCORPORATED'S SMITH CORONA TYPEWRITER WAS ENGRAVED BY GEORGE LAMBERT OF AMERICAN BANK NOTE COMPANY; (UPPER RIGHT) SOUTHLAND ICE COMPANY'S ICE BLOCK AND TONGS WAS ENGRAVED BY WALTER FRAUZ OF SECURITY BANK NOTE COMPANY; (LOWER LEFT) O'SULLIVAN RUBBER CORPORATION'S HEELS USED IN SHOE MAKING; AND (LOWER RIGHT) AMERICAN THREAD COMPANY'S SPOOL OF THREAD WAS ENGRAVED BY EDWIN GUNN OF AMERICAN BANK NOTE COMPANY. COURTESY GEORGE LABARRE (TOP LEFT AND RIGHT) AND STREBE PAPER COLLECTIBLES (BOTTOM LEFT AND RIGHT).

33 percent, and then by 75 percent more in the fall. Meat production among the Swifts, Armours, and Wilsons slowed to a trickle. A *Time* magazine survey of 139 cities found only six without meat shortages.

As the shortages became more severe, public pressure to remove the controls increased. The OPA, itself a bureaucratic monster served by seventy-three thousand people, seemed to be losing its grip. It became clear that farmers, consumers, corporations, and politicians detested controls. Finally, in a national radio address on the evening of October 14, 1946, President Truman announced the end of price controls. That same year he broke strikes in the rail and coal industries. A year later

scratching their heads was how fast to decompress. In January 1946, President Truman asked Congress for another year of the Office of Price Administration and a sixty-five-cent-an-hour minimum wage. He wanted to lift price controls, commodity by commodity, based on supply and demand. The Truman administration still didn't know what to do with the American farmers, who were miffed by a set-aside order that required them to sell the government one-half of the wheat they grew. It was acceptable during wartime, but after August 1945 it threatened rural independence. Within months the control system was near collapse, reeling from producer backlash. Meat became a rare commodity as ranchers kept cattle off the market because of low prices. In the summer of 1946 the cost of living rose

TOP LEFT: MERCURY, THE ROMAN MESSENGER OF THE GODS, MUSES OVER AN AMERICAN AIRLINES PLANE IN THIS VIGNETTE FROM THE COMPANY'S CERTIFICATE. BELOW, THE ALLEGORICAL FIGURE OF COMMERCE HOLDS A BOLT OF CLOTH ON THE J.C. PENNEY SHARE. COURTESY STOCK SEARCH INTERNATIONAL (TOP) AND STREBE PAPER COLLECTIBLES (BOTTOM).

Congress passed the Taft-Hartley labor law over Truman's veto. (This law prohibited unfair union practices.) Food prices in 1947 jumped 40 percent. New Yorkers were still paying five cents for a subway ride and a Ford coupe cost $1,300. Factory workers were earning an average of $50.42 a week compared with $42.46 a week in 1946. A school teacher was making ends meet on $2,424 a year. Radio still dominated the airwaves with the likes of Jack Benny, Fibber McGee and Molly, Fred Allen, and Walter Winchell along with music programs, soap operas, and kids shows whose sponsors

ESTABLISHED 1837.

TRADE MARK.

No 2823

This Certifi

entitled

THE

transf

The holders of

quarterly out of the

such dividends shall be cumulative, ba

to the foregoing. The shares of this Pref

CINCINNATI,
TRANSFERS.

EGISTRATION.

included Philco, RCA, Bakelite, City Services, Brunswick, Palmolive, Atwater Kent, Texaco, AT&T, Firestone, Procter & Gamble, American Tobacco, Kellogg, and Ovaltine. And a new electronic gimmick called television was starting up: There were only eighteen TV stations and one hundred and fifty thousand television sets in all of the United States.

Advertising was becoming a growth industry and so was America's mass awareness of Madison Avenue, thanks, in part, to best-selling novel *The Hucksters*, written by Frederic Wakeman, a navy veteran. (The motion picture starred Clark Gable.) Although public relations had its pallid beginnings in the 1920s, it did not gain wide acceptance until after the war, when a skeptical public recognized that the big corporations had the power to grow.

Nowhere was that growth more apparent than in the automobile industry, where the pent-up demand for product was enormous. If it had wheels, people were willing to buy it. Some thirty-two wannabe car makers announced new models—Gregory, Davis, Playboy, Scarab, Keller, Del Mar, Tucker, Kaiser, and Frazer were among them. Nearly all of them were dream machines that never saw the dawn of production. Only Kaiser, which went into production in the summer of 1946, was the first and last serious domestic challenge to Detroit's car makers since World War II. By 1947 Kaiser-Frazer raced to number four behind General Motors, Chrysler, and Ford, but well ahead of Studebaker, Nash, Hudson, Packard, Willys, and Crosley. Auto pioneer Henry Ford, who had been born during the Civil War and outlived his son, Edsel, was eighty-two when World War II

ended and his company fell from its number-one position to a distant third in 1946 production behind General Motors and Chrysler. Near senility, he was still in control of a disintegrating company. But his grandson, Henry II, who reorganized and cleaned house of stodgy and autocratic managers, coupled with the momentum of a nation hungry for wheels, revived the company's fortunes in the subsequent decades of the century. By 1950 Ford secured itself as the nation's second biggest producer, but would never overtake General Motors.

By 1949, there were four million Americans out of work while the nation's ten auto makers were producing more than five million new cars a year. A nickel could get you a ride on a streetcar or bus in Atlanta, Kansas City, and Detroit and in most cities with a public transportation network. A Saturday matinee of Hopalong Cassidy, Gene Autry, and a Flash Gordon serial cost a quarter. The United States managed to ratify the North Atlantic Treaty Organization (NATO) pact while conceding the communists victory in China. On September 20, the Dow Jones Industrial Average slumped to 178.04 from 206.97, the level it had reached in February of 1946. And the wave of African Americans migrating out of the South for the promise of jobs in the North continued: Between 1915 and 1970 more than five million headed for the larger northern cities.

In June 1950, North Korean troops invaded South Korea and the United States and the United Nations rallied to South Korea's defense. War was bullish for markets. Americans were already suffering a case of the jitters from

ABOVE: CORPORATIONS LEARNED EARLY THAT STOCK SCATTERED WIDELY AMONG SMALL INVESTORS REQUIRED A SMALLER PERCENTAGE OF THAT STOCK TO CONTROL A COMPANY. THAT'S WHY MANY BIG COMPANIES SOUGHT THE SMALL SPECULATOR. EQUALLY IMPORTANT WAS THE COLLECTIVE BUYING POWER OF THEIR CONSTITUENCIES. A BIG POOL OF STOCKHOLDERS IS ALSO A BIG POOL OF POTENTIAL CUSTOMERS, AND THAT'S WHY COMPANIES SUCH AS FRUIT OF THE LOOM (FOUNDED 1851), QUAKER OATS (1901), AND GERBER PRODUCTS (1901) IMPRINTED BRAND LOGOS ON THEIR STOCKS. COURTESY GEORGE LABARRE (TOP, CENTER) AND STOCK SEARCH INTERNATIONAL (BOTTOM).

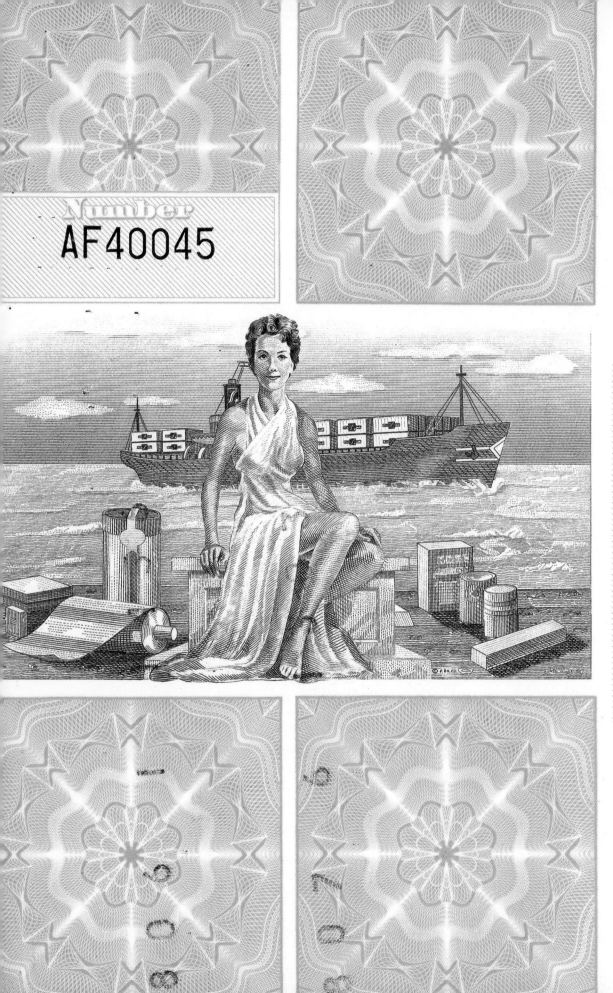

RJR

Series A Cum

Preferred S

THIS CERTIFIES THAT

is the owner of

Fully paid and non

transferable on the books of th

endorsed. This certificate and

of Incorporation of the Compan

This certificate is not valid, un

Witness the seal of the Con

LESS THAN 100 SHARES

LESS THAN 100 SHARES

NUMBER
NO76697

SHARES
-5-

PAN AMERICAN AIRWAYS CORPORATION

INCORPORATED UNDER THE LAWS OF THE STATE OF DELAWARE

THIS CERTIFICATE IS TRANSFERABLE IN THE CITY OF NEW YORK OR IN SAN FRANCISCO, CAL.

This certifies that

FIVE

is the owner of

FULL PAID AND NON-ASSESSABLE SHARES, OF THE PAR VALUE OF TWO DOLLARS AND FIFTY CENTS ($2.50) EACH, OF THE CAPITAL STOCK OF PAN AMERICAN AIRWAYS CORPORATION

transferable in person or by duly authorized attorney upon surrender of this Certificate properly endorsed. This Certificate is issued subject to all the terms of the Corporation's Certificate of Incorporation as amended and By-Laws as amended (copies of which are on file at the office of the Transfer Agent) to which reference is hereby made with the same effect as if they were herein set forth in full and to all the provisions of which the holder hereof by acceptance of this Certificate assents.

This Certificate is not valid until countersigned by the Transfer Agent and registered by the Registrar.

Witness the seal of the Corporation and the signatures of its duly authorized officers.

Dated **DEC 12 1946**

REGISTERED: THE NEW YORK TRUST COMPANY, REGISTRAR
BY
AUTHORIZED SIGNATURE.

COUNTERSIGNED: BANKERS TRUST COMPANY, TRANSFER AGENT.
ASSISTANT SECRETARY.

Pan American Airways Corporation

H. Preston Morris SECRETARY

J. T. Trippe PRESIDENT

PAN AMERICAN AIRWAYS CORPORATION CORPORATE SEAL 1923 DELAWARE

SECURITY BANKNOTE COMPANY

TENS UNITS
1 1
2 2
3 3
4 4
5 5
6 6
7 7
8 8
9 9
0 0

PAN AMERICAN AIRWAYS CORPORATION

ABOVE: PAN AMERICAN AIRWAYS CORPORATION (1946) INAUGURATED THE FIRST INTERNATIONAL AIR SERVICE BETWEEN HAVANA, CUBA, AND KEY WEST, FLORIDA AND IN TWO YEARS BECAME THE LARGEST AIR TRANSPORT COMPANY IN THE WORLD. THE CERTIFICATE SHOWS A VIGNETTE WITH A BALD EAGLE APPROPRIATELY SPREADING ITS WINGS OVER TWO HEMISPHERES. COURTESY OF STREBE PAPER COLLECTIBLES.

the end of World War II, when the Soviet Union gobbled down half of Europe with an arsenal that had three times as many airplanes and four times as many troops as the United States. For $2,000 you could build an underground cubicle in your backyard in case the Cold War turned into a hot one with both sides hurling atomic bombs at each other. And coal miners settled a strike to earn $14.75 a day.

While some people were burrowing beneath the ground, the industrial landscape was changing rapidly. Some of the very industries that had made cities like St. Louis and Chicago commercial powerhouses were dying. The biggest victim was the once venerable meat-packing industry. The regional stockyards in places like Omaha and Kansas City were vying for the title of major meat market at the end of the decade. In 1954, the Chicago stockyards celebrated the sale of their one-billionth animal. Five years later, the *Chicago Tribune* sadly observed: "Chicago, which Carl Sandburg celebrated as hog butcher to the world, isn't killing enough hogs these days to feed its own citizens." The Chicago packers were dropping like cattle on a slaughtering line. In June 1953, Swift ceased its meat-packing operations, which had been going on since 1875. Two years later, Wilson was out of business, and in

July 1959 Armour phased out. Modern communications and transportation had caught up with meat packers, who had been in business as long as Chicago was the nation's preeminent rail terminus. But by the 1950s, farmers could catch the daily livestock quotes on their radios and within hours were hauling their animals by truck to the local slaughterhouse. No longer was there a need for a central city like Chicago. But that would fast change. The airlines—United, American, Pan Am, TWA, Delta, and Braniff—replaced the

ABOVE: TWO VIEWS OF THE HISTORY OF FLIGHT. THE VIGNETTE ON THE LEFT APPEARS ON THE SHARE OF GATES LEARJET. AT RIGHT IS A BIPLANE, CIRCA 1920, FROM A GREAT LAKES AVIATION SHARE. A COMPANY PROSPECTUS OF THE TIME CITED THE NEED TO PROVE THAT AVIATION WAS A COMMERCIALLY VIABLE ENTERPRISE. COURTESY STREBE PAPER COLLECTIBLES (LEFT) AND STOCK SEARCH INTERNATIONAL (RIGHT).

railroads, carrying people instead of livestock and turning such cities as Chicago, Dallas, and Atlanta back into hubs. Barges still floated on the Mississippi and the trains still hauled cargo, but most of it was carried by the big semis crisscrossing the 41,000 miles of new interstate highways that were built in the late 1950s and 1960s.

BETHLEHEM STEEL STOCK VIGNETTES: FOUR DECADES OF CORPORATE GROWTH

ABOVE: FOUR FACES OF BETHLEHEM STEEL. OVER THE YEARS, THE VIGNETTES OF BETHLEHEM STEEL'S STOCK CERTIFICATES REFLECTED A CHANGE IN THE TIMES AND THE NATURE OF ITS BUSINESS. IN 1949, AN ALLEGORICAL SYMBOL OF HEAVY INDUSTRY WAS FLANKED BY SHIPS AND STEEL FOR RAILROADS. IN 1956, TWO EXECUTIVES LOOK OVER FUTURE PLANS WITH A MODEL OF MARTIN TOWER, BETHLEHEM'S NEW HEADQUARTERS, IN THE FOREGROUND. A CERTIFICATE ISSUED IN 1972 SPORTS A TRIO OF MANAGERS WHO WORK TO PRODUCE RAW STEEL. THE CURRENT CERTIFICATE, REVISED IN 1989, RENDERS BETHLEHEM A MODERN EMPLOYER WITH AN ARRAY OF PRODUCTS THAT INCLUDE ROLLED STEEL AND STEEL PLATE. ALL COURTESY OF GEORGE HEWITSON COLLECTIBLES.

No. 9
The First National Bank of Chicago, Illinois,
50 SHARES.
SHARES $ 100 EACH.

This Certifies

that *James C. Fargo* of *Chicago Ill.*
is entitled to *Fifty S_____* Shares of the Capital Stock
of the FIRST NATIONAL BANK OF CHICAGO, which Shares are transferable only upon the Books of
the Company at their Office in Chicago by the said *James C. Fargo*
or *by* Attorney upon surrender of this Certificate.
Dated Chicago, this *25th* day *June* 186*3*

Cash*r*   Pres*t*

Lith by Ed. Mendel, 162 Lake St. Chicago.

Know all men by these presents that I *James C. Fargo of Chicago Ill*
do truly appoint _____ to be _____ true and lawful
Attorney to sell and transfer the whole or any part of *Fifty*_____ Shares
in the Capital Stock of the First National Bank of Chicago with power to nominate one or
more persons under him, and to do all necessary acts to accomplish that purpose.
Witness _____

THE FIRST NATIONAL BANK OF CHICAGO, ILLINOIS

ABOVE: THIS STOCK CERTIFICATE, OF THE FIRST NATIONAL BANK OF CHICAGO, ILLINOIS, WAS ISSUED IN 1863 TO JAMES FARGO, WHO SUCCEEDED HIS BROTHER, WILLIAM, AS PRESIDENT OF AMERICAN EXPRESS COMPANY IN 1881.

THE BANK'S PATRIOTISM DURING THE CIVIL WAR IS OBVIOUS FROM THE CERTIFICATE'S CORNER VIGNETTES: A UNION SOLDIER AND THE AMERICAN EAGLE. ALSO NOTE THE REVENUE STAMP WITH GEORGE WASHINGTON'S FACE AT LOWER

LEFT. TO HELP PAY FOR THE CIVIL WAR, THE FEDERAL GOVERNMENT PASSED A LAW IN 1862 THAT PLACED A SMALL TAX ON ALL FINANCIAL TRANSACTIONS THAT INVOLVED CHECKS, DEEDS, STOCKS, AND BONDS. COURTESY OF GEORGE LABARRE.

NUMBER
SS204558

SHARES
1000

COMMON STOCK

COMMON STOCK

BankAmerica Corporation

INCORPORATED UNDER THE
LAWS OF THE
STATE OF DELAWARE·

THIS CERTIFIES THAT

THIS CERTIFICATE IS
TRANSFERABLE IN
SAN FRANCISCO
OR LOS ANGELES

IS THE OWNER OF

SEE REVERSE FOR
CERTAIN DEFINITIONS

SS204558   1000   066050 10 5

ONE THOUSAND

CUSIP 066050 10 5

FULL-PAID AND NON-ASSESSABLE SHARES OF THE PAR VALUE OF $3¹²⁵ EACH OF THE COMMON STOCK OF
BANKAMERICA CORPORATION, transferable in person or by duly authorized attorney upon
surrender of this certificate properly endorsed. This certificate is not valid unless countersigned
by the Transfer Agent.
Witness the facsimile signatures of the duly authorized officers of the corporation.

Dated: MARCH 31, 1972

CERTIFICATE OF STOCK

COUNTERSIGNED:
BANK OF AMERICA
NATIONAL TRUST AND SAVINGS ASSOCIATION
(SAN FRANCISCO)   TRANSFER AGENT

BY

AUTHORIZED OFFICER

SECRETARY

RESIDENT

© SECURITY-COLUMBIAN BANKNOTE COMPANY

SEP 25 1974

A28375

B49599

INTERNATIONAL BUSINESS MACHINES CORPORATION

ABOVE AND OPPOSITE: IBM HAS BEEN MAKING PRODUCTS FOR COMPUTING AND TABULATING SINCE 1911. FOUR YEARS LATER THOMAS WATSON WAS RUNNING THE COMPANY. BY THE TIME HIS SON, TOM WATSON, JR. BECAME CEO IN 1956, TRANSISTORS HAD REPLACED VACUUM TUBES. AS COMPUTERS BECAME SMALLER IBM GREW INTO THE WORLD'S LARGEST COMPUTER MANUFACTURER WITH NEARLY THREE HUNDRED THOUSAND EMPLOYEES IN MORE THAN ONE HUNDRED COUNTRIES. THE VIGNETTES ON THE SHARES SHOWN ABOVE (TOP: 1958 AND BOTTOM: 1969) ARE EMBLEMATIC OF THE TRANSITION. COURTESY OF R.M. SMYTHE & CO., INC. (TOP) AND KEN PRAG PAPER AMERICANA (BOTTOM).

100 SHARES

100 SHARES

C 508132

C508132

NUMBER

CBS INC.

100

SHARES

INCORPORATED UNDER THE LAWS OF THE STATE OF NEW YORK
DOMESTIC SHARE CERTIFICATE
SEE REVERSE FOR CERTAIN DEFINITIONS AND RESTRICTIONS

This certifies that

PEN NOM 699-790 & CO

COUNTERSIGNED AND REGISTERED CHEMICAL BANK
TRANSFER AGENT AND REGISTRAR

AUTHORIZED SIGNATURE

is the owner of

CUSIP 124845 10 8

ONE HUNDRED

COMMON

fully paid and nonassessable shares of the Common Stock of
CBS Inc., transferable on the books of the Corporation by the holder hereof in person or by
duly authorized attorney on surrender of this certificate properly endorsed.
This certificate is not valid unless signed by Transfer Agent and registered by Registrar.
Witness the signatures of the Corporation's duly authorized officers.

Dated   JULY 22 1975

TREASURER

PRESIDENT

CBS Inc.

Above: A year after United Independent Broadcasters Inc. went public in 1927, the Paleys, a Chicago family, put up $400,000 for a stake in the fledgling New York radio network. Back then, the two-year-old NBC network dominated the airwaves. Subsequently UIB's name was changed to Columbia Broadcasting System, and over the next fifty years, William Paley made radio and television history in building one of the nation's largest and most profitable networks. Today CBS is owned by Westinghouse. The certificate shown here is from 1975. Courtesy of George LaBarre.

S59632

CERTIFICATE FOR LESS THAN 100 SHARES

CERTIFICATE FOR LESS THAN 100 SHARES

NUMBER

00000

SHARES

WARNER BROS. PICTURES, INC.

INCORPORATED UNDER THE LAWS OF THE STATE OF DELAWARE

This Certifies that _____

is the owner of _____ full-paid and non-assessable shares WITHOUT NOMINAL OR PAR VALUE, OF THE COMMON STOCK of Warner Bros. Pictures, Inc. (hereinafter called the "Corporation") transferable on the books of the Corporation by the holder hereof in person or by duly authorized attorney, upon surrender of this certificate properly endorsed. A description of the different classes of stock of the Corporation and a statement of the relative rights of the holders of stock of such classes is printed upon the back hereof, and this certificate and the shares represented hereby are issued and shall be held subject to all of the provisions of the Certificate of Incorporation of the Corporation and of the amendments thereto (copies of which are on file with the Transfer Agent) to all of which the holder by the acceptance hereof assents. This certificate is not valid until countersigned by the Transfer Agent and registered by the Registrar.

In Witness Whereof, Warner Bros. Pictures, Inc. has caused this certificate to be signed by its duly authorized officers.

Dated _____

SPECIMEN Thomas. SECRETARY.

SPECIMEN Werner, PRESIDENT.

REGISTERED: MANUFACTURERS TRUST COMPANY, REGISTRAR.

AUTHORIZED OFFICER

COUNTERSIGNED: THE NEW YORK TRUST COMPANY, TRANSFER AGENT.

ASSISTANT SECRETARY:

TENS UNITS
1 1
2 2
3 3
4 4
5 5
6 6
7 7
8 8
9 9
0 0

AMERICAN BANK NOTE COMPANY.

WARNER BROS. PICTURES, INC.

ABOVE: The allegorical muses of entertainment flank the Warners Brothers film studio in the vignette on this unissued Warner Bros. Pictures, Inc. stock certificate. Incorporated in 1923, the studio made movie history by 1927 when it released *The Jazz Singer,* the first "talkie" that featured sound in musical numbers sung by Al Jolson. For decades the company was run by Jack Warner, one of the legendary titans in Hollywood's so-called golden age of film when the autocratic Louis B. Mayer and Irving Thalberg roamed the studio lots. Courtesy of George LaBarre.

CORPORATED UNDER THE LAWS OF THE COMMONWEALTH OF PENNSYLVANIA

This Certifies that

By 1969 a human being had walked on the moon, the Saturday Evening Post ended publication after 148 years, and a new word appeared in the business lexicon—conglomerate. A conglomerate was an assemblage of unrelated businesses under one corporate roof, and its builders were called conglomerators. Perhaps no one captured the essence of this new c.orporate device better than a hardscrabbling Texan named James Ling, who by the end of the decade had outmaneuvered the trust busters to parlay his conglomerate, LTV Corporation (Ling Temco Vought), into a $3.7 billion entity, putting him ahead of such giants as Du Pont, Shell, and Westinghouse in terms of sales.

THE NEW CONGLOMERATES

Ling had combined the sixth largest steel company (Jones & Laughlin), the eighth-largest airline (Braniff), the eighth-largest defense contractor (Chance Vought), the third-largest meat packer (Wilson & Co.), the largest sporting-goods maker (Wilson Sporting Goods Co.), and a string of others in a random group of industries. The strategy allowed conglomerates to grow quickly with an immediate stream of profits and revenues. In essence, it was a means of shortcutting the old-fashioned way of earning money through plodding research, development, and the marketing of new products. Now a conglomerate with its diverse and instant product line could withstand the shocks of business cycles that made single-product companies vulnerable. Other conglomerates of the era included ITT, Gulf and Western, Northwest Industries, Litton Industries, and Loew's, each run by equally colorful, ambitious, single-minded, and shrewd CEOs like Harold Geneen, Charles Bluhdorn, Ben Heineman, and Laurence Tisch.

In addition to the conglomerators, the sixties could also claim the so-called go-go managers of mutual funds. The "go-go" referred to the gyrations of the funds, which darted in and out of stocks, concentrating on the short-term performance of newer and more speculative issues rather than the ven-

OPPOSITE: TRACING ITS ROUTES BACK TO 1899, VF CORPORATION, MAKER OF LEE AND JANTZEN, CHANGED ITS NAME FROM VANITY FAIR MILLS IN 1969. PUBLIC SHARES WERE FIRST OFFERED IN 1951. THE VF VIGNETTE WAS ENGRAVED BY JOHN WALLACE, JR. FOR AMERICAN BANK NOTE. COURTESY LES KRANTZ.

erable blue chips. In his book titled *Ling*, Stanley Brown, an astute and witty observer of America's business scene, summed it up this way: "Mutual funds used to be nice things for widows and orphans to invest in; they weren't supposed to be hot stocks, just safe ones. Then came along people like Gerald Tsai, and the funds were performing like uranium stocks in the good old days. But when it appeared that there was nothing much holding many of them up except zeal, they collapsed, along with the market, or ahead of it, in some cases."

The market downturn of the seventies pretty much ended the mischief of the go-go funds and briefly slowed the merger mania. For one company to buy another with its stock, the market must be viable. Bull markets are great for acquisitions because they generally raise the value of a company's stock. During bear markets, if a company's stock falls in lockstep with the rest of the market, it will hibernate until the market springs back. That happened in the late 1970s when the nation was wracked by high interest rates, high unemployment, high inflation, and a seesawing stock market that sank the Dow Jones industrial average to a low of 750. The New York Stock Exchange wasn't the only game in town. By the mid-1970s there was an exchange and a smorgasbord of products for nearly every investment taste.

Among a host of smaller exchanges was New York's American Stock Exchange that traded in the stocks of primarily the younger, smaller, and more volatile companies. And there were the regional exchanges in Boston, Philadelphia, Chicago, Cincinnati, and San Francisco, as well as a host of commodities exchanges. In Chicago, in addition to the Midwest Stock Exchange, there were the Chicago Board of Trade, the nation's oldest commodity exchange founded in 1848, the Chicago Mercantile Exchange, which traced its roots to 1874, and a relative newcomer, founded in 1972, the Chicago Board Options Exchange, the only exchange that traded options on stocks. (An option allowed an owner to buy a set number of common shares at a set price on or before a set date.)

Trading in the over-the-counter market (OTC) had greatly expanded in 1970 with the innovative creation of NASDAQ (National Association of Securities Dealers Automated Quotation System), a fully computerized quotation system. The OTC market is a widespread aggregate of dealers who make markets in many different securities ranging from Microsoft common stock to government bonds. Unlike an exchange where trading takes place at one physical location, the OTC market connects buyers and sellers through the telephone and computer. Today NASDAQ lists the securities of 4,934 public companies and the NYSE lists 3,098 companies. But keep in mind that an exchange sets no prices, it only mirrors the economy. And without buyers and sellers it languished like other sectors.

Not even the bicentennial and the tall ships that glided through New York harbor could distract people from the harsh economic realities of the times. The auto industry felt the brunt of competition and began to lay off workers as foreign cars grabbed nearly 30 percent of the U.S. market. The ripple effect spread to other industries as many of the nation's steel mills—and the towns that grew around them—were turning into crumbling museums of a different industrial age. The term "rust bowl" was being used to describe areas in the Midwest like East Chicago and Gary, Indiana, where the once fiery mills of U.S. Steel were shut down and abandoned, leaving their hulks decaying like scattered skeletons of cattle that had perished in their tracks during a drought.

During the seventies, American companies operating overseas began to realize the new monetary world demanded a broad foreign exchange market. In 1972, for instance, Americans were watching the Olympics from Munich through the ABC network, which was losing $2 million because someone apparently overlooked a simple fact: The network was collecting receipts and paying its bills in two different currencies, dollars and Deutsche marks. ABC hadn't bothered to hedge its foreign exposure against the potential risk of adverse fluctuations in the Deutsche mark. To do so it would have had to buy so-called currency futures contracts that locked in the current price of the Deutsche mark for delivery at a future date. In essence, a futures contract is an insurance policy of a kind, permitting people to lock in a guaranteed future price for a commodity or a financial instrument.

For years, farmers along with companies like Coca-Cola, General Mills, Kraft, Nabisco, Pillsbury, ITT, Cargill, Central Soya, Archer Daniels Midland, and Continental Baking, had bought and sold commodities contracts to hedge the prices of the raw products they used. If, for example, Coca-Cola feared sugar prices were going to rise in the winter months ahead, it bought futures contracts that guaranteed delivery of sugar in the spring at today's prices. Since

the mid-nineteenth century the use of futures contracts enabled everyone from the Illinois soybean farmer to the giant Minneapolis grain trading concern to the Boston baker to the Texas cattle rancher to make educated forecasts. But in the early 1970s few companies had dipped their toes into the murky waters of currency hedging, and the use of futures contracts with arcane terms like spreading, hedging, straddles, butterflies, shorts, and longs seemed like a new kind of jive talk, a lingo with a pornographic ring.

ABC wasn't the only multinational corporation that hadn't mastered the ABCs of foreign exchange. Earlier, for example, Cheseborough-Pond's had attained record sales and earnings despite increased losses on foreign exchange, equivalent to nearly 5 percent of its net income. Farm machinery maker John Deere & Company, in its 1971 annual report, included a ten-year summary of consolidated income showing write-offs for foreign exchange losses for every year since 1962, ranging from hundreds of thousands of dollars to millions. F.W. Woolworth in 1967 wrote off nearly $3 million, or the equivalent of about 6 percent of its income, while Proctor & Gamble found it necessary in 1971 to increase its reserves for foreign operations because of currency volatility. In 1974, Gulf Oil lost $25 million on one of its foreign loans.

There were, of course, success stories, too. Outboard Marine Corporation attributed earnings gains to foreign exchange trading, as did Hewlett Packard, Ford, McDonald's, and Kodak, as well as some of the major banks including Bank of America, Citicorp, Chase Manhattan, and Morgan

Guaranty. The smart companies, however, were careful not to depend on foreign exchange operations as profit centers, but solely as hedging vehicles to protect profits. There was little doubt that the need for financial markets was being expressed when, in 1979, the New York–based firms of Salomon Brothers, Goldman Sachs, and Discount Corporation became members of the Chicago Mercantile Exchange, where its International Monetary Market division would become a marketplace for trading contracts on foreign currencies, stock index futures, and such interest rate–sensitive financial instruments as Treasury Bills and Eurodollars.

Inflation continued to play havoc with investors in 1981. The financial storm began when Federal Reserve chairman Paul Volcker announced an increase in the discount rate—the interest rate charged on borrowings by member banks—of a full point to 12 percent, and an increase in the reserve member banks held. The development touched off turmoil in the money markets. Interest rates soared higher and billions of dollars in securities values were wiped out. By the year's end interest rates rose to 15 percent. In his determination to end high inflation, Volcker squeezed harder, sending the prime rate to 21.5 percent in early 1981.

Stock market investors chasing higher returns sold their stocks and poured billions into money market funds, whose assets jumped from $77 billion to $190 billion. Like a summer tornado, recession tore through the economy. Housing sales, auto sales, and corporate profits tumbled. The Dow skidded from 1,024 in April to 820 in September. Outsiders invaded Wall Street, taking over Shearson, Bache,

Salomon Brothers, and Dean Witter Reynolds. It was the beginning of the economy of the 1980s, distorted and inflated by leveraged buyouts, massive high-yield, unsecured junk-bond issues, vast fusions of credit, and the sale of a Van Gogh painting for an astonishing $53.9 million.

The nation's financial community was given another jolt with the failure of Penn Square Bank in Oklahoma that set off a shock wave of write-offs among such big-city lenders as New York's Chase Manhattan and Chicago's Continental Illinois Bank (now part of BankAmerica), which nearly collapsed from the more than $1 billion in Penn Square oil loans it had purchased. Continental was rescued by the Federal Deposit Insurance Corporation, but its ambition to become a world-class money-center bank was considerably pared down. On the plus side, Congress managed to cut the capital gains holding period from one year to six months, while Great Britain cut oil prices, resulting in a worldwide oil glut. All along, the federal deficit crept up.

Better times for the stock market were just around the corner, but it didn't seem that way in early 1982. The economy was shaky from the worst economic setback since the 1930s as unemployment rose above 10 percent, imperiling dozens of companies with bloated borrowing and energy costs. The Volcker recession began to ease during the summer, when the discount rate was cut three times, a clear indication that interest rates in mortgages and auto loans were likely to go lower in the months ahead. That's all it took to ignite the stock market. On August 12th the Dow bottomed out and over the next five days climbed almost 100 points.

The bull market of the 1980s was underway along with an emerging intermarket system—where trading takes place between two or more markets—in futures and options. No longer did a money manager have to dump a stock portfolio or sell off $500 million in bonds to adjust a position. In the course of a day, a corporate treasurer could trade Eurodollars in Chicago, Brent crude oil futures in London, and Japan's Nikkei stock index futures in Singapore. And even if a treasurer never traded a futures contract directly, chances were good that his or her banker did to offset risk.

With stock market averages down 10 to 20 percent at one point in 1983, before they rebounded on the plus side, the flexibility and low cost of stock index futures looked attractive. A stock index future contract called for the future delivery of a sum of money based on the value of a stock index, like the Standard & Poor's 500 stock index or the Dow Jones group of stocks. The index contract enabled investors to speculate on the future direction of the stock market rather than on just a few stocks. Or the institutional investor could hedge a portfolio of securities against general market movements. The strategy caught on and by mid-1983 some 123 of the three hundred largest domestic and foreign banks operating in the United States were using futures. Similarly, pension funds—which accounted for the indirect stock market participation of most people—loomed as serious users of futures as well. An annual survey by *Pensions and Investment Age* revealed that twenty-six public and corporate pension funds used futures in 1983, double the number that did in 1982. Among the new pension players were American Can, Atlantic Richfield,

Chrysler, Delta Airlines, Grumman Corporation, IBM, Phillips Petroleum, Sears Roebuck, and Texaco. A couple of the most enlightened users of stock index futures were the General Motors Corporation pension fund and the Harvard Management Company, which managed Harvard University's huge endowment fund, the largest in the United States.

The insurance companies, too, were following suit: Within the year, ten states, including California, Illinois, New York, and Virginia, passed legislation that struck down barriers to using futures. In New York, for example, insurance companies were given the nod to hedge 2 percent of total assets; in California, 5 percent; and in Illinois, futures positions were linked to a company's capitalization. In just over a decade, financial futures had caught on with amazing speed. In 1983, among all U.S. exchanges, 140 million contracts had changed hands, compared to 17.3 million in 1972. More than one third of futures trading in 1983 involved financial instruments, stock indexes, and foreign exchange.

By late summer 1984, the U.S. economy was becalmed and the stock market had inched back up, but not until after the nation's financial system was somewhat shaken by several events. Earlier in the year, AT&T had spun off its seven regional operating companies under an antitrust settlement. Shortly thereafter, both Volcker and Martin Feldstein, President Reagan's top economic advisor, cast gloomy forecasts for the economy. The result: Stocks fell again, sending the Dow average below 1,100. After the Dow was up 12 percent in 1982 and 20 percent in 1983, it closed down 3.7 percent at the end of 1984.

For investors in the stock market, 1985 was a year of confusion. Early in the year, the dollar had ceased its long climb against other currencies. With Japanese long-term bond rates at 7 percent and the Tokyo stock market trading at around thirty times earnings, American investors turned their attention to international mutual funds and foreign markets. The action on Wall Street continued to be fueled by the free-market fury of leveraged buyouts and takeovers like General Electric's acquisition of RCA. The realities of supply and demand had also grabbed the world's cartels. Attempts to fix prices in tin, cocoa, rubber, sugar, and coffee failed. Competition even forced the Organization of Petroleum Exporting Countries (OPEC) to shed is price-fixing oil strategy like an outdated wardrobe.

Meanwhile, the foreign exchange markets were sending a clear message: The United States was a threadbare trillionaire living beyond its means—and could no longer continue to do so. The key was the negative balance of trade. Only a positive balance would mean greater demand for a country's currency. Because the dollar is the world's reserve currency and principal means of international exchange, the world's other industrialized nations had but one choice: to push the dollar down. By early September the dollar had fallen 23 percent against the Deutsche mark, 33 percent against the British pound, and 10 percent against the Japanese yen.

By 1986 the stock market was still pushing skyward. But a tragic start to the new year occurred in January, when the space shuttle *Challenger* exploded before the eyes of millions of viewers shortly after liftoff. An explosion of another kind rolled Wall Street in the following months as the Securities and Exchange Commission began a series of insider trading inquiries against a group of hard-driving, high-earning investment bankers. All the while the dramatic rise in the stock market strained the logic of the most astute analysts. How high could the market go? In January, the Dow industrial average soared to 1,600. In February, it passed 1,700; in March, 1,800. At mid-year the average stood at 1,900. Most analysts were convinced that the great bull market of the 1980s would continue to charge into the next decade with, of course, a correction or two along the way. Looming on the financial horizon in 1986 was the tantalizing prospect of the Dow reaching 2,000.

In the summer of 1986, Ling's stitched-together LTV Corporation unraveled. LTV filed for bankruptcy, listing liabilities of nearly $4.25 billion, including some $2.2 billion in long-term debt. Typical of a company with little cash, LTV did junk-bond financing. In short, it sold unsecured bonds that paid investors a high rate of return to pay for LTV's acquisitions. For investors, it was high-risk deal. For LTV it meant high-interest payouts it couldn't afford. In a four-month period the price of the bond had dropped in market value from $700 to $200 and investors received no interest income during the reorganization.

The very next year, the stock market itself would come apart. Despite the Dow's record breakthrough in January 1987, there lingered traces of uncertainty as to where the market was heading. Having seen it pass the 2,000 barrier, investors wondered, Would it be propelled to greater heights?

CERTIFICATE FOR NOT MORE THAN 10,000 SHARES

CERTIFICATE FOR NOT MORE THAN 10,000 SHARES

COMMON STOCK

COMMON STOCK

XEROX
CORPORATION

INCORPORATED UNDER THE LAWS OF THE STATE OF NEW YORK

THIS CERTIFICATE IS TRANSFERABLE IN NEW YORK CITY, IN ROCHESTER, N.Y., IN CHICAGO, ILL. OR IN SAN FRANCISCO, CAL.

SPECIMEN

SEE REVERSE FOR CERTAIN DEFINITIONS

This is to Certify that _____ is the owner of

CUSIP 984121 10 3

FULL-PAID AND NON-ASSESSABLE SHARES OF THE COMMON STOCK OF

XEROX CORPORATION *transferable on the books of the Corporation by the holder hereof in person or by duly authorized attorney, upon surrender of this certificate properly endorsed. This certificate and the shares represented hereby are issued and shall be held subject to all of the provisions of the Certificate of Incorporation, as amended of the Corporation (a copy of which Certificate is on file with the Transfer Agent), to all of which the holder by acceptance hereof assents. This certificate is not valid until countersigned by the Transfer Agent and registered by the Registrar. Witness the signatures of the duly authorized officers.*

Dated:

REGISTERED: MORGAN GUARANTY TRUST COMPANY OF NEW YORK, REGISTRAR,

AUTHORIZED OFFICER.

BY

TREASURER.

CHAIRMAN OF THE BOARD.

COUNTERSIGNED: FIRST NATIONAL CITY BANK, TRANSFER AGENT

AUTHORIZED OFFICER.

BY

AMERICAN BANK NOTE COMPANY.

XEROX CORPORATION

ABOVE: INCORPORATED IN 1906 AS THE HAROLD COMPANY, BY 1958 IT WAS KNOWN AS HAROLD XEROX, INC. THREE YEARS LATER, IT WAS SIMPLY THE XEROX CORPORATION, PLAYING OFF ONE OF THE BEST KNOWN TRADEMARKS IN AMERICAN HISTORY. IN FACT, THE COMPANY ACTUALLY EMPLOYED A NOMENCLATURE STRATEGY BY REGISTERING THE TRADEMARK XEROX (DERIVED FROM THE GREEK *XEROS*, MEANING DRY), THEN COINING THE RELATED GENERIC TERM XEROGRAPHY TO DESCRIBE THE DRY COPYING PROCESS. THE UNISSUED SHARE'S ALLEGORICAL VIGNETTE OF SCIENCE AND INDUSTRY WAS ENGRAVED BY AMERICAN BANK NOTE COMPANY. COURTESY GEORGE LABARRE..

Or would it fizzle? After a five-year bull market wasn't a correction due? In all the fervor over market mania, most people had forgotten what happened to the Dow when it passed the 1,000 historic benchmark in 1982. It took a decade before it cracked 1,100. But there was even more fodder for fretting. By the summer of 1987, the United States was fidgeting on a bed of economic travails that included a lackluster economy, sliding interest rates, a weak dollar, and ballooning trade and budget deficits. Fundamentals aside, there were international tensions of the day that included falling prices on foreign stock markets and squabbling among countries over the exchange rates of their currencies. The investment sages couldn't agree about how much life was left in the bull market. While some saw rainbows, others saw clouds of recession gathering. Yet the Dow reached 2,722 in August. As it turned out, that was the peak.

On Monday, October 19, came the crash that was heard around the world when the stock market suffered its worst single-day decline in history. The Dow's Black Monday plunge of 22.6 percent was the largest one-day drop ever, almost doubling the record of the 12.8-percent fall on October 26, 1929. By the time the Dow closed the day at 1,738.74, more than $500 billion—a sum equal to the entire gross national product of France—had vanished. After a five-year run the stock prices could no longer ignore the air of unreality that swept over the market like a plume of stale cigar smoke. Based on interest rates, sub-par corporate earnings, and other fundamentals, lamented some analysts, the market several months before the crash had moved higher on sheer greed.

The crash also served as a reminder that trading patterns had changed over the years, rendering the small investor a minnow in an ocean of whales. The technology of the 1980s offered institutional investors—mutual funds, pension funds, endowment funds, and trust departments, for example—a scale and a sophistication they could not resist. The big institutional players now dominated the market and they could buy and sell huge blocks of stocks and other securities, causing them to fluctuate during short periods of time. In the early 1980s selling or buying more than thirty stocks at one time was the trading art of the day. By the mid-1980s trading in subsets of the five hundred different stocks was routine. And so was program trading—computer-aided strategies that automatically kicked in buy and sell orders at certain price points. For example, one program-trading strategy is tactical asset allocation, which employs stocks, bonds, futures, options, and cash equivalents. Through a predetermined formula and programmed computers, one asset is exchanged for another to get the highest yield from an investment portfolio.

Before the crash, there was a general feeling in the United States that, given the lessons of history learned from the 1929 crash, coupled with the money, brains, and tech-

OPPOSITE: THE PULITZER PUBLISHING COMPANY AND SEATRAIN LINES EMPLOY SIMILAR ALLEGORIES TO TELL DIFFERENT STORIES ON THEIR SHARE CERTIFICATES. BOTH WERE ETCHED AND PRINTED BY AMERICAN BANK NOTE COMPANY. COURTESY STREBE PAPER COLLECTIBLES (TOP) AND GEORGE LaBARRE (BOTTOM).

nology circulating in the world of finance, disaster could be avoided. But it seemed that a crash wasn't all that different from a tornado—if the conditions are right, there's no stopping it, even if you see it coming. Both are spontaneous outbursts and both spread devastation and ruin. Apparently, the precise mixture of emotions and events created the right conditions in 1987. In any event, the crash of 1987 sent a clear message: The global financial system—locked in a maze of immense institutions and intricate trading strategies— and its players were fallible. Markets remain volatile for one reason and one reason only: too many unanswered questions, and too many unanticipated events—like the one that took place in 1989 and that reminded Wall Street of the market's hair-trigger temper.

In the two years after the crash the market regained its composure with pre-crash zeal. On October 9, 1989, the Dow Jones industrial average hit a record peak. Four days later, however, the Dow plunged 190.58 points, or 6.91 percent, making it the second-biggest point drop ever, surpassed only by the 508-point loss recorded on Black Monday two years before. The spark that had lit the market's fuse, analysts later suggested, was the failure of a UAL Corporation (the parent of United Airlines) buyout group to secure financing for the deal. On Monday, October 16, even before the analysts could complete their damage assessments of Friday's market, the Dow rebounded 88.12 points—the fourth-largest point-gain ever.

Exchange officials viewed the Friday sell-off as a litmus test for the post-crash reforms that had been designed to accommodate heavy trading and discourage panic-selling.

The plunge had set off the so-called circuit breakers—a trading halt—that were put in place under a signed agreement between the Chicago Mercantile Exchange and the New York Stock Exchange after the 1987 crash. The circuit breakers were to provide the market with a cooling-off period, a chance to give the markets time to regain their equilibrium. On Friday, the Merc's circuit breakers had kicked in and trading was halted for thirty minutes, breaking the link between the futures and stock markets. On Monday, the NYSE, in anticipation of massive selling orders, opened its computers one hour earlier than usual to help sort out business before trading began. The crash proved that the futures markets had become an integral part of the financial markets and now the exchanges were working in tandem to preserve order.

At the beginning of 1990, the market tried to regain its composure as companies and consumers began to work off the vast debt they had assumed in the 1980s. Economists were predicting at least several years of modest growth in productivity before American industry could rebuild its long-term future and bring prosperity back, though never, some insisted, back to the prosperity of the 1960s—not with the kind of staggering budget deficit hanging over the nation. The markets, manic one minute, depressed the next, reacted to the economic blahs as 1990 unfolded.

Across the Atlantic, Western Europe was busy positioning itself economically for the twenty-first century with the formation of the European Union. Napoleon's fantasy of uniting the states of Europe would begin to take shape hopefully within two years when twelve nations became one market of three hundred and twenty million people with the "invisible hand" reaching across European borders to touch every facet of life from patent law to the pedigree of bovine animals. Goods, services, labor, and capital were to move freely in this boundary-less economic world, which had a single aim: to counter the industrial might of the United States and Japan. The last golden age of European economics that bloomed in the 1960s had wilted by the early 1970s from overzealous regulation, nationalistic squabbling, trade bickering, recessionary shocks, Bretton Woods, and oil jolts. Now a barrier-free market—with a common currency tying it together—had endless possibilities.

While Western Europe was building its economic future, Eastern Europe was dismantling its political past, struggling to realign itself into a pre-World War II map. With the collapse of the Berlin Wall between the two Germanys, and the Baltic States search for independence, the Cold War was in the throes of rapid deconstruction. The dissolution of the communist system would eventually spread to the Russian homeland itself during 1990, shattering the myth that capitalism would forever remain isolated. Now there existed the possibility that perhaps capitalism could become the dominant system of organizing humans' economic activities. Capitalism even managed to climb the Asian steppes to Ulan Bator, the capital of Mongolia, where every Tuesday shares of five formerly state-owned companies changed hands on the Mongolian Stock Exchange. The land of Genghis Khan, squeezed between Russia and China, had come full circle: in 1921 Mongolia had become the first Asian country to embrace communism, and in 1990 it was the first Asian country to let go of communism.

Just as the summer of 1990 was winding down, two matters sprung upon the world, neither of which was a pleasant prospect: Iraq's invasion of Kuwait and the onset of a recession. The invasion would lead to the Gulf War and a sweeping victory calculated in hours—too quickly for troops to sustain battle fatigue. Unfortunately, the economic fight on the home front looked more like a case of chronic fatigue. The recession lingered; weeks turned to months, months to years. It became the longest, if not the deepest, downturn since the Great Depression. The war didn't cause the recession, but it was being blamed for the growing economic woes as the price of oil spurted from twenty dollars to forty dollars a barrel, sending gasoline prices at the pump to their highest levels ever. A savings-and-loan crisis was already in full swing and the real estate market was severely depressed when President Bush dispatched troops to the Middle East. The usual terms crept into the economists' rhetoric, including "sluggish," "lethargic," and "lackluster," to describe a traumatized economy in which 1.2 million workers lost their jobs in the first eighteen months.

It would get worse. In January 1991 alone, another 232,000 workers were laid off. By then some thirty states were deep in debt and were ready to tax everything from personal incomes to pretzels. Eastern Airlines, Continental, and Pan Am (which subsequently folded along with Midway Airlines) had filed for bankruptcy protection under Chapter 11. More layoffs would follow as such industry giants as General Motors, IBM, AT&T, and Citicorp began to restructure them-

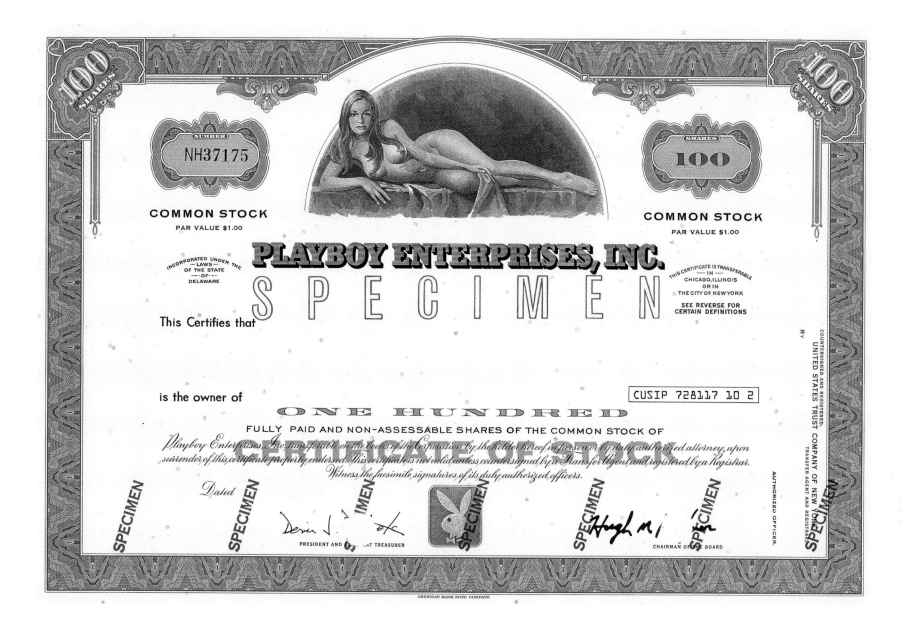

NUMBER
NH37175

COMMON STOCK
PAR VALUE $1.00

COMMON STOCK
PAR VALUE $1.00

SHARES
100

PLAYBOY ENTERPRISES, INC.

INCORPORATED UNDER THE
—LAWS—
OF THE STATE
—OF—
DELAWARE

SPECIMEN

THIS CERTIFICATE IS TRANSFERABLE
—IN—
CHICAGO, ILLINOIS
OR IN
THE CITY OF NEW YORK

SEE REVERSE FOR
CERTAIN DEFINITIONS

This Certifies that

is the owner of

CUSIP 728117 10 2

ONE HUNDRED

FULLY PAID AND NON-ASSESSABLE SHARES OF THE COMMON STOCK OF

Playboy Enterprises, Inc. transferable on the books of the Corporation by the holder hereof in person or by duly authorized attorney, upon surrender of this certificate properly endorsed. This certificate is not valid unless countersigned by a Transfer Agent and registered by a Registrar. Witness the facsimile signatures of its duly authorized officers.

CERTIFICATE OF STOCK

Dated

PRESIDENT AND ASSISTANT TREASURER

CHAIRMAN OF THE BOARD

COUNTERSIGNED AND REGISTERED:
UNITED STATES TRUST COMPANY OF NEW YORK
TRANSFER AGENT AND REGISTRAR

BY

AUTHORIZED OFFICER.

AMERICAN BANK NOTE COMPANY.

PLAYBOY ENTERPRISES, INC.

ABOVE AND OPPOSITE: Called *FEMALE NUDE*, THE PLAYBOY ENTERPRISES VIGNETTE, SHOWN HERE IN A CIRCA 1980 COMMON STOCK CERTIFICATE, WAS CREATED BY ARTIST ROBERT LAVIN, A FORMER ILLUSTRA-TOR FOR THE *SATURDAY EVENING POST* AND *READER'S DIGEST*. HIS PAINTINGS ARE IN THE PERMANENT COLLECTION OF THE SMITHSONIAN INSTITUTION. THE ENGRAVER IS WARRELL HAUCK. LAVIN CREATED FIFTY-FIVE PIECES OF ART FOR THE AMERICAN BANK NOTE COMPANY FOR VARIOUS CERTIFICATES, FOURTEEN OF WHICH WERE ENGRAVED BY HAUCK. COURTESY OF GEORGE LABARRE.

175

STOCK

$1.00

ER THE

PLAYBOY ENTER

S P E C I

es that

selves to play out the 1990s in the name of increased efficiencies and reduced costs. Such survival strategies—praised by Wall Street analysts because they made a company's bottom line more attractive—became a stake of fear driven through the hearts of America's work force, white- and blue-collar alike. Not since the 1930s had the threat of unemployment hung over the nation on such a large scale.

The nagging recession was forcing more people to turn their backs on the American dream and its post–World War II promise of prosperity. Ironically, the two pillars that had so dominated the psyche of most Americans since the late 1940s—the belief in ongoing prosperity and the crusade against communism—were crumbling at the same time. Trapped by a Federal deficit, steep taxes, declining income, and higher housing costs, the sons and daughters of middle-class families began to talk about fewer opportunities than their parents had enjoyed. College graduates were faced with the poorest employment prospects in years and many took on menial jobs with hopes that the job market would eventually loosen up. Others polished their academic resumes and headed for crowded graduate schools in order to enhance their credentials while waiting out the recession. But there was hardly any relief in sight. In their frenzied strategies to downsize and improve profits, U.S. companies, economists predicted, would be shedding more than one million jobs in 1992—a presidential election year ("It's the economy, stupid!" became Bill Clinton's war-room cry).

Soured by hard economic realities, consumer confidence waned, despite the Fed's cut in the discount rate, which helped inch fixed-rate mortgages downward. The drop in rates resulted in a wave of asset allocation, a shifting or diversification of assets. With low yields on CDs and Treasury securities, investors put money into the stock market: a record $34 billion flowed back into mutual funds in 1991. That kind of money turned the stock market defiant to the point of ignoring the heavy debt on the economy and the signs of a protracted recession. By December 1991, short-term interest rates were the lowest in twenty-seven years, triggering a rally that sent the stock market to record heights. For the year the Dow Jones average rose 535 points—more than a 20 percent gain—to a record peak of 3,168.83. The S&P 500 leaped even more than the Dow during the year, rising 26 percent, and NASDAQ, the barometer for small stocks, jumped a record 57 percent. It was as if the focus on market volatility since the crash had turned from fear to fascination.

By the close of the nineties, the downturn had reversed itself just as it had done in the previous eight recessions since World War II. The Dow was back to setting new records, having blown through 10,000. Now analysts were giddy with predictions, talking about 25,000 sometime in the next century. In early 1999 unemployment was at its lowest level since 1970, while rising incomes and steadily declining mortgage rates helped keep new housing starts on a record pace. Home remodeling had become a $130 billion business nationwide, surpassing new home building in dollar volume. The United States was a good neighbor, having bailed out Mexico in its financial crisis. And with severe recession plaguing most Asian and Latin American countries, and with Japan's economy in disarray, America's markets were attracting foreign investors, which fueled the rally. The dollar was strong, the budget balanced, the Fed was keeping a close reign on interest rates, and America was flush with investment capital. What better time for private companies to go public and public companies to sell more stock—and to buy up other companies.

If anything, the emergence of the conglomerate back in the sixties demonstrated a fact of corporate life that would carry to the end of the twentieth century and will likely go on through the next as well: almost every widely held corporation in America is vulnerable to a takeover—friendly or otherwise.

Thanks to the bull markets of the 1990s, deregulation of various industries, and the federal government's relaxed antitrust posture, economic Darwinism returned to Wall Street: Survival of the fittest became the vogue of financiers and once again giantism became desirable. That attitude fit in with America's laissez-faire message to the rest of the world: free markets for free people. Even the big media, which covered the machinations of the merger phenomenon over the years, came under merger attack. Big newspaper chains gobbled up smaller ones. Independent magazines became the target of media moguls, as did major book publishers. They, in turn, were bought up by film studios, who ended up in the portfolio of modern conglomerates. Today CBS is owned by Westinghouse, NBC by General Electric, ABC by Disney, and CNN by Time Warner—blurring the lines, say critics, between journalism and entertainment. Wall Street itself traded in its independence for a price-earnings ratio. Such

financial institutions as American Express and insurance firms like Traveler's have snapped up brokerage houses and investment-banking firms, while investment bankers like Morgan Stanley merged with brokerages like Dean Witter, creating an impressive stream of revenues and profits along with a string of names, making them sound more like law firms. The big banks became giant banks by taking over other big banks: the merger of Citicorp and Chase and of Bank of America and Nations Bank are among them.

Higher stock prices also have fostered the growth of new businesses, providing numerous opportunities for millions of investors, while encouraging a rash of Initial Public Offerings (IPOs) among small startup companies as well as old-line ones that have spun off key operations as part of a streamlining strategy. In October 1998, for example, Conoco, which had been a part of DuPont since 1981, offered $4.4 billion of its stock to the public—the biggest IPO issue in American history. Or consider PepsiCo, whose chief product, Pepsi-Cola, has been battling Coca-Cola in literally a hundred-year-old cola war. In a two-year restructuring plan, PepsiCo sold off its fast-food chains that included Pizza Hut, Taco Bell, and Kentucky Fried Chicken (KFC) and then, in March 1999, it spun off its main $7 billion bottling operation into an independent public company—the same move made by Coke years earlier to create Coca-Cola Enterprises. In the meantime, the castoffs—KFC, Pizza Hut, and Taco Bell— became a separate company called Tricon Global Restaurants, with more outlets worldwide than McDonald's and annual sales of $8.5 billion.

SHARES $100 EACH

No. 781

Be it known that

is the Proprietor of

Capital Stock of the Bank

each, which Stock is transferabl

said Richard Delafi

or his Attorney on surrender

of the said Bank.

Witness

Cashier

AFTERWORD

Today there is a swaggering energy in the economy—just as in America's past economies when there were plenty of jobs, inflation was nil, the dollar was respected worldwide, and people were generally optimistic about their future prospects. That optimism is reflected in the stock market, where trillions slosh in and out daily buying and selling the IBMs, General Electrics, and Polaroids of tomorrow. New companies are the lifeblood of America's economy. It's the small companies, with their entrepreneurial flair, that employ most of the nation's workers and have been the innovators. Don't forget that IBM didn't market the first personal computer; Apple Computer did when it was a fledgling company in a place in northern California called Silicon Valley.

Today the darlings are known simply as Net stocks, a reference to those publicly-held companies that are cashing in by providing services on the Internet. These are companies like Amazon.com, the on-line bookseller that bills itself as the biggest bookstore in the world and whose market value exceeds that of Sears. Yet, in January 1999 Amazon was losing money. And there was eBay, the on-line auctioneer that went public in September 1998; within four months its stock had jumped tenfold, making it six times as big as the venerable old-line auction house of Sotheby's. When Netscape Communication's merger with America

Online was initially announced in November 1998, the deal was worth some $4 billion. By April 1999, the deal's value had ballooned to $15 billion because of AOL's soaring stock price. Netscape was one of the hottest start-ups in history when it was launched in January 1995, but it was battered by the much bigger Microsoft in the browser wars. When Microsoft started distributing Internet Explorer free, Netscape lost its main source of revenue and had to change its strategy by developing new products.

That's how it goes in the Net economy, which, as *Newsweek*'s Brad Stone put it, "is being built one triumphant IPO at a time." But is it a house of cards? "Without question," observed *Time*'s money columnist Daniel Kadlec. "Internet stocks are the hottest things since biotechnology shares soared in 1991 (and crashed in 1992), and may be the hottest things since the Dutch

tulip-bulb craze in the 1600s." Or perhaps the frenzy over Net stocks may indeed be part of a fleeting trend in an economic cycle. The late Harvard economist Joseph Schumpeter believed technical innovation was the key to economic cycles. Once the technology had matured, he argued, the decline began. The era of the Iron Horse, for example, produced investment and prosperity. But after the railroads had been built, investment dropped sharply, causing a downswing. He explained it in 1942 in *Capitalism, Socialism and Democracy*: "The process of industrial change," he wrote, "provides the ground swell that gives the general tone to business....Thus there are prolonged periods of rising and falling prices, interest rates, employment and so on, which phe-

nomena constitute parts of the mechanism of this process of recurrent rejuvenation of the productive apparatus." For the majority of today's stock market investors, cycles and Schumpeter hold about as much appeal as do quantum mechanics and particle physics. Instead, when it comes to finding the market's grail, opinions vary as much as approaches and methods. Some rely on sci-

OPPOSITE: THE FEMALE ON PEPSICO'S STOCK CERTIFICATE (CIRCA 1971) IS THE IMAGE OF WORLDLINESS COMPARED TO HER 1834 COUNTERPART (ABOVE) FROM THE DELAWARE & RARITAN RAILROAD CERTIFICATE. COURTESY STREBE PAPER COLLECTIBLES (OPPOSITE) AND GEORGE LABARRE (ABOVE).

ence and mathematics; others on tips, systems, hunches, bluffs, calculated chances, and the power of quick intuition. More than a few resort to the stars and even to prayer. Like philosophers in search of some truth that binds all mankind, the market analysts, technicians, and fundamentalists keep striving, all sharing a common belief: There is something in the market system that weaves everything together, something that can be calculated, something that can respond to high-tech input that short-circuits human nature or reproduces it—in a financial world that merges, dissolves, and oscillates like cells in some complex structure.

Yet no one has come up with a foolproof way to beat the market's odds or even, for that matter, to calculate them. Perhaps the market is a chimera, a mythological beast that never really exists except in the mind. Stocks are stocks. And they will either go up or down. It's been that way as long as there have been markets. Only the names and pockets have changed—along with the face on the stock certificate.

SOURCES

Atlanta Numismatics and Currency
PO Box 20173
Atlanta, GA 30325
tel. (404) 351-7960

David M. Beach
PO Box 2026
Golden Rod, FL 32733
tel. (407) 657-7403
fax (407) 657-6382

George Hewitson Collectibles
PO Box 975
Engelwood, FL 34295
tel. (941) 475-4181
fax (941) 474-9630

Ken Prag Paper Americana
PO Box 14817
San Francisco, CA 94114
tel. (415) 586-9386

LaBarre Galleries, Inc.
PO Box 746
Hollis, NH 03049
tel. (1-800) 717-9529
fax (603) 882-4797

R. M. Smythe & Co.
26 Broadway
New York, NY 10004
tel. (212) 943-1880
fax (212) 908-4047

Stock Search International, Inc.
4761 W. Waterbank Drive
Tucson, AZ 85741
tel. (520) 579-5635
fax (520) 579-5639

Strebe Paper Collectibles
PO Box 793
Seabrook, MD 20703
tel. (301) 794-6054

Scripopholy Magazine
The International Bond & Share Society
15 Dyatt Place
PO Box 430
Hackensack, NJ 07603-0430
tel. (201) 489-2440
fax (201) 592 0282

SELECTED BIBLIOGRAPHY

Ackerman, Kenneth D. *The Gold Ring.* New York: Dodd, Mead & Company, 1988.

Adams, Henry. *The Education of Henry Adams.* Boston: Houghton Mifflin, 1930.

After the Crash. Washington, D.C.: American Enterprise Institute for Public Policy Research, 1988.

Allen, Frederick Lewis. *Only Yesterday: An Informal History of the 1920's.* New York: Harper & Row, 1964.

————. *Since Yesterday 1929-1939.* New York: Perennial Library, 1972.

Berkow, Ira. Maxwell Street: *Survival in a Bazaar.* New York: Doubleday & Company, 1977.

Birmingham, Stephen. *Our Crowd.* New York: Harper & Row, 1967.

Braun, Hans, ed. *Historic Stock Certificates USA.* Berlin: Verlag Hermann Schmidt Mainz, 1996.

Brealey, Richard A., and Myers, Stewart C. *Principles of Corporate Finance.* New York: The McGraw-Hill Companies, 1996.

Brouwer, Kurt. *Mutual Funds.* New York: John Wiley & Sons, 1988.

Brown, Stanley H. *Ling.* New York: Atheneum , 1972.

Burgess, Anthony. *The Great American Cities/New York.* New York: Time-Life Books, 1976.

Cameron, James. 1914. *New York:* Rinehart, 1959.

Cleaver, Dale G. *Art An Introduction.* New York: Harcourt, Brace & World, 1966.

Cochran, Thomas C., and Miller, William. *The Age of Enterprise: A Social History of Industrial America.* New York: Harper & Brothers, 1961.

Collier, Peter, and Horowitz, David. *The Fords.* New York: Summit Books, 1987.

Cooper, Wendy A. *Classical Taste in America 1800–1840.* New York: Baltimore Museum of Art, Abbeville Press, 1993.

Cowen, Tyler. *Program Trading: A Look Behind the Headlines.* Irvine, Calif.: Citizens for a Sound Economy Foundation, 1988.

Cowing, Cedric B. *Populists, Plungers, and Progressives: A Social History of Stock and Commodity Speculation, 1890-1936.* Princeton: Princeton University Press, 1965.

Cox, Terry. *Stock And Bonds of North American Railroads.* Port Clinton, Ohio: BNR Press, 1995.

Dedmon, Emmett. *Fabulous Chicago.* New York: Random House, 1953.

Dooley, Martin. *Mr. Dooley in Peace and War.* Boston: Small, Maynard, 1898.

Durand, John. *The Life And Times of A.B. Durand.* New York: Kennedy Graphics/Da Capo Press, 1970.

Elson, Robert T. Time Inc. *The Intimate History of a Publishing Enterprise 1923–1941.* New York: Atheneum, 1968.

Falater, Lawrence. *American Automobile Stock Certificates.* Port Clinton, Ohio: BNR Press, 1997.

Flint, Jerry. *The Dream Machine.* New York: Quadrangle, 1976.

Friedman, Milton, and Schwartz, Anna Jacobson. *A Monetary History of the United States, 1876–1960.* Princeton: Princeton University Press, 1963.

Galbraith, John Kenneth. *The Great Crash: 1929.* Boston: Houghton Mifflin, 1961.

Garbani, James H. *Arizona Mines And Mining Companies.* Tucson: Arizona Territorial Trader, 1993.

Gastineau, Gary L. *The Options Manual.* New York: McGraw-Hill, 1988.

Glennon, Lorraine, ed. *Our Times The Illustrated History Of The 20th Century.* Atlanta: Turner Publishing, 1995.

Goldman, Eric F. *Rendezvous with Destiny: A History of Modern American Reform.* New York: Random House, 1956.

Goulden, Joseph C. *The Best Years: 1945–1950.* New York: Antheneum, 1976.

Griffiths, William H. *The Story of American Bank Note.* New York: American Bank Note Company, 1959.

Gunther, John *Roosevelt in Retrospect: A Profile in History.* New York: Harper & Brothers, 1950.

Halberstram, David. *The Fifties.* New York: Villard Books, 1993.

Halberstram, David. *The Powers That Be.* New York: Knopf, 1979.

Harris, Neil. *The Artist in American Society: The Formative Years, 1790-1860.* Chicago: University of Chicago Press, 1982.

Heise, Kenan, and Edgerton, Michael. *Chicago: Center for Enterprise. Vols 1& 2.* Woodland Hills: Windsor Publications, 1982.

Hendy, Anne-Marie. A*merican Railroad Stock Certificates.* London: Stanley Gibbons Publications, Ltd, 1980.

Hessler, Gene. *An Illustrated History of U.S. Loans.* Port Clinton, Ohio: BNR Press, 1988.

Hessler, Gene. *The Comprehensive Catalog of U.S. Paper Money.* Port Clinton, Ohio: BNR Press, 1995.

Hessler, Gene. *The Engraver's Line.* Port Clinton, Ohio: BNR Press, 1993.

Hicks, John R. *The Crisis in Keynesian Economics.* Oxford: Blackwell, 1974.

Hill, John, Jr. *Gold Bricks of Speculation.* Chicago: Lincoln Book Concern, 1904.

Hofstadter, Richard. *The Age of Reform: from Bryan to FDR.* New York: Knopf, 1955.

Hollander, Keith. *Scripophily.* New York: Museum of American Financial History, 1994.

Holmes, Oliver Wendell, Jr. *The Common Law.* Boston: Houghton Mifflin, 1881.

Howe, Irving, and Libo, Kenneth. *How We Lived: A Documentary History of Immigrant Jews in America, 1880-1930.* New York: Plume, 1979.

Jackson, Kevin. *The Oxford Book of Money.* New York: Oxford University Press, 1995.

Johnson, Allen, and Malone, Dumas, eds. *Dictionary of American Biography.* New York: Charles Scribner's Sons, 1958.

Johnson, Paul. *The Birth of the Modern (World Society 1815–1830).* New York: HaperCollins, 1991.

Keynes, John Maynard. *The General Theory of Employment, Interest and Money.* New York: Harcourt Brace Jovanovich, 1936.

Lefevre, Edwin S. *Reminiscences of a Stock-Operator.* Garden City, N.Y.: Garden City Publishing, 1923.

Leuchtenburg, William E. *The Perils of Prosperity, 1914–32.* Chicago: University of Chicago Press, 1958.

Lowe, David. *The Great Chicago Fire.* New York: Dover, 1979.

Lurie, Jonathan. T*he Chicago Board of Trade, 1859-1905: The Dynamics of Self-Regulation.* Urbana: University of Illinois Press, 1979.

MacKay, Charles. *Extraordinary Popular Delusions & the Madness of Crowds.* New York: Crown, 1980.

Magee, John. *The General Semantics of Wall Street.* Springfield, Massachusetts: John Magee, 1964.

Manchester, William. *The Glory and the Dream, Vols. 1& 2.* Boston: Little, Brown, 1973, 1974.

Mayer, Martin. *Markets.* New York: W.W. Norton, 1988.

———. *The Fate of the Dollar.* New York: Signet, 1981.

Melville, Herman. *Moby Dick.* Cambridge, Massachusetts: Riverside Press, 1956.

Morgan, Dan. *Merchants of Grain.* New York: Viking Press, 1979.

Nachman, Gerald. *Raised on Radio.* New York: Pantheon Books, 1998.

Peters, Edgar. "Portfolio Insurance or Asset Allocation or Both?" The Boston Company, 1987.

Predergast, Curtis, with Colvin, Geoffrey. *The World of Time Inc. The Intimate History of a Changing Enterprise 1960–1980.* New York: Atheneum, 1986.

Reinfeld, Fred. *The Story of Civil War Money.* New York: Sterling Publishing, 1959.

Rolfe, Sidney E., with Robert G. Hawkins. *Gold and World Power.* New York: Harper & Row, 1966.

Rose, Barbara. *American Art Since 1900.* New York: Frederick A Praeger, 1967.

Rothbard, Murrray N. *America's Great Depression.* Los Angeles: Nash Publishing, 1972.

Samuelson, Paul A. *Economics: An Introductory Analysis.* New York: McGraw-Hill, 1961.

Schaaf, Barbara C. *Mr. Dooley's Chicago.* New York: Anchor Press/Doubleday, 1977.

Schlesinger, Arthur M., Jr. *The Age of Roosevelt: Crisis of the Old Order.* Boston: Houghton Mifflin, 1957.

Scott, David L. *Wall Street Words.* Boston: Houghton Mifflin, 1988.

Shannon, David A., ed. *The Great Depression.* Englewood Cliffs, N.J.: Prentice-Hall. 1960.

Shell, Marc. *Money, Language, And Thought.* Baltimore: The Johns Hopkins University Press, 1982.

Sinclair, Upton. *The Jungle.* New York: Signet Classics, 1964.

Sobel, Robert. *Panic on Wall Street: A Classic History of America's Financial Disasters—with a New Exploration of the Crash of 1987.* New York: E.P. Dutton, 1988.

Steffens, Lincoln. *The Autobiography of Lincoln Steffens.* New York: Harcourt, Brace, 1931.

Strange, Susan. *Casino Capitalism.* Oxford: Basil Blackwell, 1986.

Swanberg, W.A. *Jim Fisk: The Career of An Improbable Rascal.* New York: Charle Scribner's Sons, 1959.

Tamarkin, Bob. *The New Gatsbys.* New York: William Morrow, 1985.

——————. *The Merc.* New York: HarperBusiness, 1993.

Taylor, Joshua, C. *Learning to Look.* Chicago: University of Chicago Press, 1981.

Time-Life Books. *The Cowboys.* New York: Time-Life Books, 1973.

Time-Life Books. *The Railroaders.* New York: Time-Life Books, 1973.

Time-Life Books. *This Fabulous Century. Prelude: 1870-1900; Vol. 6: 1950-1960; Vol. 7: 1960-1970.* New York: Time-Life Books, 1971.

Veblen, Thorstein. *The Theory of the Leisure Class.* New York: The Viking Press, 1945.

Wall, Joseph, Frazier. *Andrew Carnegie.* New York: Oxford University Press, 1970.

Ward, Geoffrey C. *The West.* Boston: Little, Brown, 1996.

Weil, Gordon L., and Davidson, Ian. *The Gold War: The Story of the World's Monetary Crisis.* New York: Holt, Rinehart and Winston, 1970.

White, Eugene N., ed. *Crashes And Panics.* Homewood, Illinois: Dow-Jones Irwin, 1990.

SELECTED PUBLICATIONS

Darby, Mary. "In Ponzi We Trust." *Smithsonian,* December, 1998.

Dyer, Davis, Kantrow, Alan, M. "The First Tycoon." *Business Month,* July/August 1988.

Maclean, John N. "Steel Yard Blues." *Chicago Tribune Magazine,* March 29, 1992.

Sanger, David E. "Global Markets' Role Widens." The *New York Times,* October 20, 1987.

Standish, David. "The Art of Money." *Smithsonian,* August 1998.

Sterngold, James. "The Events That Changed the World of Wall Street." The *New York Times,* October 26, 1987.

Stewart, James B., and Hertzberg, Daniel. "Terrible Tuesday: How the Stock Market Almost Disintegrated A Day After the Crash." The *Wall Street Journal,* November 20, 1987.

Tomasko, Mark D. "Two Hundred Years of American Bank Note Company." Museum of American Financial History brochure, 1999.

Wallich, Henry C. "The Dollar Viewed from Abroad." Newsweek, August 30, 1971.

White, Peter T. "The Power of Money." *National Geographic,* January 1993.

"Who's in Charge? The Crash on Wall Street Spotlights America's Leadership Crisis." *Time,* November 9, 1987.

Zweig, Jason. "Wild Pitch: How American Investors Financed The Early Growth of Baseball." *Financial History,* Summer, 1997.